Ornamental Aquarium Fish of India

Kishori Lal Tekriwal and
Andrew Arunava Rao

KINGDOM

© 1999 Kingdom Books, PO Box 15, Waterlooville PO7 6BQ, England.

Contents

dedication

Umang Tekriwal, born 14 November 1975, died 19 April 1996.

This book is dedicated to the fond and loving memory of our dearest son and founder partner, who was an inspiration in all our work in the Indian aquarium tropical fish scene.

His indefatigable energy, patience, wit and humour and, above all, his tremendous support both to his father as well as his working partner at all times made him an example which both of us and our respective families can never forget.

Umang Tekriwal to whom this book is dedicated.

acknowledgements

We wish to thank Mr John Dawes for so kindly writing the preface of this book. We are much obliged to our photographers, Mr Jonathan Amitava Rao and Mr Shilbhadra Dutta, for their patience which has rewarded us with these rare and wonderful photographs. We are thankful to the whole staff and collectors of Aqua Decor of Calcutta, India without whose invaluable help this work could not have commenced in the first place.

And lastly we are indebted to our respective families for their support and encouragement during the production of this book.

Kishori Lal Tekriwal
Andrew Arunava Rao

foreword

My first contact with Indian fishes occurred in the late 1950s, a mere few weeks after I began keeping freshwater tropical aquarium fish. That first species was the enchanting Dwarf Gourami (*Colisa lalia*). I still remember the profound effect that the males' brilliant red and bluish body stripes had on me, but what fascinated me above all else were their long, hair-like pelvic fins and their amazing bubblenests.

Those early specimens were commercially bred, although I didn't know this at the time. It was only many years later that I cast eyes on my first genuinely wild Dwarf Gourami pairs. Their colours were not as brilliant as those of either my early Dwarves or the thousands that I had come across and bred since. They were, however, even more beautiful and fascinating, in a pure, 'unadulterated' sort of way.

My early experiences with the Dwarf Gourami led to a passionate interest in Indian and other labyrinth fishes (culminating in the presidency of the Anabantoid Association of Great Britain), as well as in Indian fishes in general. Over time, I have kept, bred and studied many of these, but have often found – like so many other similarly-minded enthusiasts and researchers – relevant information hard, or even impossible to come by. Certainly, much valuable information is available, but it is usually widely dispersed. Frequently, this worthy body of data is presented by authors who, like me, have direct experience of some of the species concerned, but have to rely on other sources to fill in the gaps.

It was therefore a great pleasure to me to meet the co-authors of this book, Kishori Lal Tekriwal and Andrew Arunava Rao, some years ago. Talking to them, seeing some of their fish and admiring their impressive photograph collections, opened up a whole new 'window' of appreciation for me into what is still, at least among aquarists. a relatively little-known species assemblage.

The idea for this book has been germinating for several years now and, like everything worth doing, could not be rushed. Research has had to be meticulous, and patience of Job-like magnitude needed in order to obtain specimens and photographs of such a large number of species. The result is a collection of Indian fish spanning 10 orders, 53 families, 119 genera and 250 species.

What makes this impressive volume particularly valuable is that, rather than provide us with just scientific/biological details (essential though these undoubtedly are), the authors have gone a significant step further by summarising the aquarium characteristics and requirements of these species and illustrating each by means of a colour photograph.

Ornamental Aquarium Fish of India therefore represents a major contribution, both as an important source of reference for ichthyologists, and as a frontier-forging publication for the international aquarium-keeping community, many (even most) members of which will be seeing a large number of these species in full colour for the very first time.

I compliment the authors on the results of their remarkable endeavours and hope that, as they gain further experience with all the many species which have been omitted owing to lack of knowledge regarding their captive care requirements, they will be able to fulfil their desire to publish a second volume of *Ornamental Aquarium Fish of India* in due course.

John Dawes
Sabinillas, Manilva, Spain

introduction

The aquarium hobby in India is nearly 70 years old. It began with the British who ruled India until 1947. In the early stages the hobby was mainly for the élite, British and Indian alike. In those times glass bowls and fancy marble pools were used to keep fish, including imported goldfish.

During the 1930s some enterprising collectors shipped to England such endemic varieties as the beautiful Dwarf Gourami, the Glass Fish and some species of Barbs. After Independence, some aquarium retail shops were formed which concentrated more on various fancy types of aquaria than on exotic fish.

At that time, the export of live wild mammals, reptiles and birds was big business, and it did not take long for entrepreneurs to start exporting freshwater tropical fish. The only drawback at that time was the transit time. Fish were sent in open metal drums by sea and there were huge casualties. This led to alternative and better packing mediums and, as a matter of course, fish were despatched by air.

Left: Fishermen casting their nets at an estuary of the Brahmaputra river, Assam.
Facing page, top: One of the 50-60 daily casts.
Facing page, bottom: The total daily catch rarely exceeds 5kg, making this very hard work with a low return.

Apart from very common species of fish which were found in abundance near major cities, nothing was done by those in the trade to survey or collect other more exotic varieties. Knowledge of Indian fish was limited to the records of the Zoological Survey of India (ZSI) which had carried out extensive work in this field, but data on whether or not these fishes were suitable for aquaria was not forthcoming. Specimens preserved in alcohol at the ZSI collections had lost their original colour and at times this led to much confusion as to their identification. Many highly scientific and technical books on Indian fish have been published, mostly by the ZSI, but no attempt has been made to depict colour photographs of live fish.

In this book we have tried to depict aquarium fish of Indian origin which should assist both the professional and the amateur icthyologist/aquarist to identify easily Indian freshwater and some brackish water fishes. It deals with 119 genera with 250 species falling under 53 families and 10 orders. It includes some of the known fresh and brackish water fishes found within the political boundaries of India, Pakistan, Bangladesh, Burma, Sri Lanka, Nepal and Bhutan.

Brief salient features of all groups have been given. In addition, we have included in simple diagrammatic form the following for each species depicted: pH, general hardiness, average length, community fish or otherwise stated, food habits, breeding habits. Maps have been included to show the geographical range of certain fish. The bibliography contains all pertinent literature of the fish dealt with in this book.

Kishori Lal Tekriwal
Andrew Arunava Rao
Calcutta

chapter 1

India

For its size, the erstwhile 'Indian Empire', or British India, contains one of the richest and most varied piscifaunas on the face of the globe. This vast sub-continent – in area two-thirds of Europe – with its extensive coastline affords suitable living conditions to a huge variety of piscean inhabitants. For biological considerations it is customary to include Sri Lanka as well as Pakistan and Myanmar.

Covering some 40 degrees of latitude and about the same of longitude, India encloses within its boundaries a vast diversity of climate and physical features. These range from the dry, scorching, sandy deserts of Sind and Rajasthan and the humid, evergreen rainforests of Assam and the southern Western Ghats, to the region of glaciers and eternal snow in the mighty Himalayas. Smooth, wide spaces of depressed river basins, either sandy, dry and sun-scorched, cultivated, or waterlogged under a steamy, moisture-laden atmosphere (the terai) lie along the base of the northern ramparts. The great Central Indian and Deccan plateaux succeed the fertile alluvial Gangetic Plain and are flanked on the west by the broken crags and castellated outlines of the ridges of the Western Ghats which overlook the Arabian Sea and continue southward in gentle, smoothly rounded slopes of green uplands – the Nilgiri and other Hills of southern India.

The area as a whole falls into the zoogeographical division of the earth known as the Oriental region. For the sake of convenience the region has been split up into five primary sub-divisions:

- the Indo-Gangetic Plain extending across the whole of northern India from the Arabian Seas to the Bay of Bengal. Its boundaries run up the hill ranges from Karachi to Peshawar, along the outer spurs of the Himalayas to Bhutan, and thence roughly southward to east of the Sunderbans. The southern boundary takes a line from the Rann of Kutch to Delhi and from about Agra to Rajmahal from where it goes south to the Bay of Bengal.
- Peninsular India, southward of the above area.
- Sri Lanka.
- the Himalayas, including the whole area of the mountain ranges from their foothills up to the limit of tree-growth.
- Assam (and Myanmar).

The Punjab, Sind and Rajasthan have a piscean fauna different from other parts of India, resembling that found in Western Asia and North Africa, whilst the fishes of the Higher Himalayas (above the tree-line) and the Upper India Valley resemble those of Central Asia. Both these areas belong to the zoogeographical region which extends over the greater part of Asia and all Europe, known as the Palearctic.

It is clearly desirable to have a further splitting of the fishes within these broad sub-divisions on the basis of ecological or environmental factors. A scrutiny shows that there is a close similarity between the flora and fauna of those regions in which the incidence of the south-west monsoon is heaviest, namely the Himalayas east of Sikkim and the hilly portions of Assam and Myanmar on the one hand, and the south-western corner of the India peninsula, south of about Goa, together with the south-western portions of Sri Lanka on the other. As a result of the similar physical configuration of all these areas and their geographical position relative to the strike of the south-west monsoon currents, these are areas of heavy rainfall and excessive humidity, two of the most important factors that regulate the character of the vegetation. Similarity in vegetation is a striking feature of these areas of heavy rainfall. As would be expected, this similarity extends to the insect forms dependent upon the plants, which in turn lead to similarity in the birds which prey upon them. It has therefore been suggested that all these parallel areas, far-flung though they be, are perhaps better lumped together in one zoogeographical subdivision.

The total area of India is 3,287,263 sq km. There is an estimated population of 844,324,222 people. The density of human population, which has been worked out on comparable data, is 267 people per sq km.

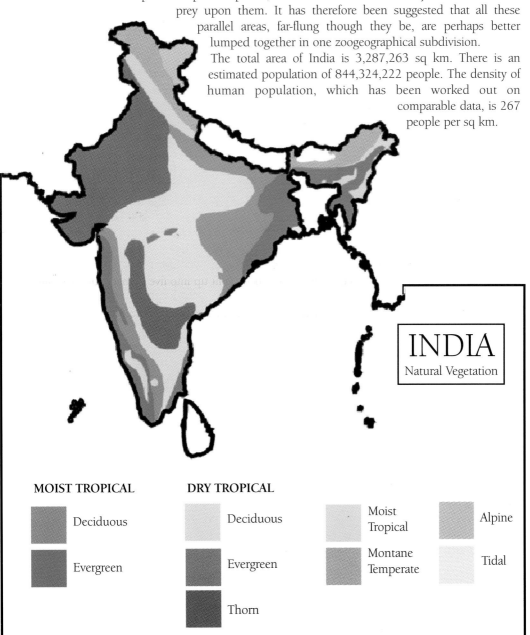

INDIA
Natural Vegetation

MOIST TROPICAL

Deciduous

Evergreen

DRY TROPICAL

Deciduous

Evergreen

Thorn

Moist Tropical

Montane Temperate

Alpine

Tidal

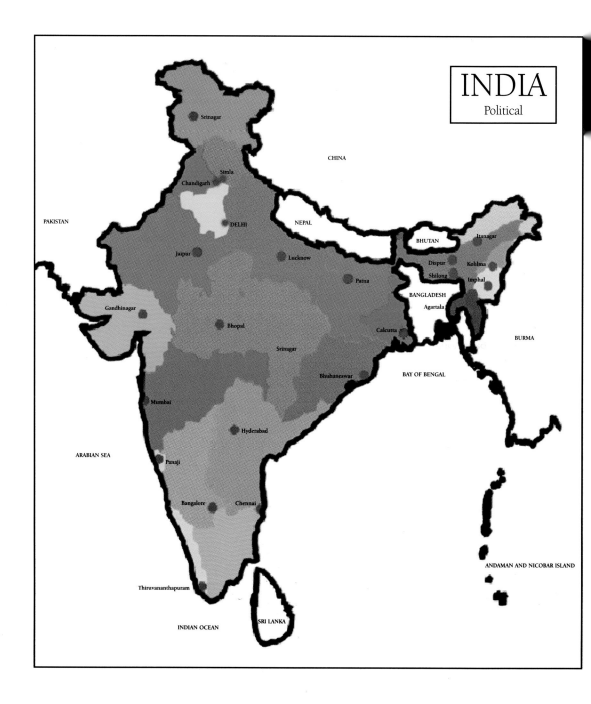

There are 26 states and 6 Union Territories in India.

ZONES	AREAS IN SQ KM.	POPULATION	DENSITY OF POPULATION PER SQ KM.
Northern Zone			
Chandigarh (UT)	114	640725	5620
Delhi (State)	1483	9370475	6319
Haryana (State) capital Chandigarh	44212	16317715	369
Himachal Pradesh (State) capital Shimla	55673	5111079	92
Jammu and Kashmir (State) capital Srinagar	222236	7718700	59
Punjab (State) capital Chandigarh	50362	20190795	401
Rajasthan (State) capital Jaipur	342239	43880640	128
Southern Zone			
Andhra Pradesh (State) capital Hyderabad	275068	66354559	241
Karnataka (State) capital Bangalore	191791	44806468	234
Kerala (State) capital Thiruvanthapuram	38863	29032828	747
Pondicherry (UT)	492	807045	1640
Tamil Nadu (State) capital Chennai	130058	55638318	428
Central Zone			
Madhya Pradesh (State)	443446	66135862	149
Uttar Pradesh (State) capital Lucknow	294411	139031130	472
Western Zone			
Dadra and Nagar Haveli (UT) capital Silvassa	491	138401	282
Daman and Diu (UT)	110	101439	906
Goa (State) capital Panaji	3704	1168622	316
Gujarat (State) capital Gandhinagar	196024	41174343	210
Maharashtra (State) capital Mumbai	307690	78748215	256

Eastern Zone

Bihar (State)	173877	86338853	497
capital Patna			
Orissa (State)	155707	31512070	202
capital Bhubaneshwar			
West Bengal (State)	88752	67982732	766
capital Calcutta			

North-eastern Zone

Arunachal Pradesh (State)	83743	858392	10
capital Tanagar			
Assam (State)	78438	22294562	284
capital Dispur			
Manipur (State)	22327	1826714	82
capital Imphal			
Meghalaya (State)	22429	1760626	78
capital Shillong			
Mizoram (State)	21081	686217	33
capital Aizawl			
Nagaland (State)	16579	1215573	73
capital Kohima			
Sikkim (State)	7096	405505	57
capital Gangtok			
Tripura (State)	10486	2744827	262
capital Agartala			

Islands

Andaman and Nicobar Islands (UT)	8249	279111	34
capiral Port Blair			
Lakshadweep (UT)	32	51681	1615
capital Kavaratti			

THE AQUARIUM TRADE IN INDIA

Aquarium fish breeding is centered around the three large cities of Mumbai, Chennai and Calcutta.

In Mumbai are the sophisticated breeders who, perhaps through lack of space caused by the very high real estate costs, have resorted to breeding small, rare and expensive fishes. This is the main Angel and Tetra breeding centre, where both small and big breeders churn out more than several hundred thousand fishes every year. Of the three cities, Mumbai lacks one essential for the aquarium fish breeder – live feeds. Live Tubifex worms are more or less extinct and Daphnia is not found in great abundance. Therefore, Mumbai breeders depend more on Brine Shrimps and other prepared foods. This has led to very healthy and disease-free fish. During the last few years major breakthroughs have been achieved in the breeding of a variety of Discus strains, Neon Tetras, Rummynose and Emperor Tetras and also Silver Dollars.

In Chennai are found the really big fish farms that devote much of their time to Mollies,

Goldfish, Koi and Lake Malawi Cichlids. Here too, there is a great shortage of live Tubifex but this is compensated for by the abundant availability of fresh live Bloodworms. Due to the city's close proximity to the sea, the bulk collection and culture of Sea Angels and other allied species have become quite popular.

Calcutta was the pioneer city of the fish breeders as most of the popular aquarium fish were first imported here and then distributed elsewhere. In this city, primarily breeding is focussed on Swordtails, Guppies and a variety of Goldfish not bred in the rest of the country. In addition there are many amateur breeders who are serious hobbyists, and who take great pains to import very rare and exotic fish from all over the world for their breeding programmes. In this city one would find breeding colonies of Six Banded Disthicodus, innumerable numbers of South American and African Cichlids and people are trying to breed the Silver Arowanas. There is an abundance of all live foods but, as there is not much education regarding proper treatment, disease is rampant among the fishes of the small-scale breeders.

A fish farm in Chennai.

Calcutta is also the main centre for the native fish export circuit. Most of the popular aquarium fish with great export demand come from the North-eastern States of India. A few of the exporters in Calcutta with very big fish farms specialise only in the culture and breeding of native wild-caught fish. Some of these export companies are also engaged in safeguarding the environment and threatened water bodies and greatly assist with their expertise and financial help.

With the strict enforcement of the Wildlife Protection Act of 1972, amended in 1980, lawful trade in all species of birds, mammals and reptiles has been banned for export as well as the local trade. This has made the aquarium fish hobby very popular and, over the last few years, over a thousand retail aquarium shops have opened throughout the country. Quite a few Clubs and Societies have also sprung up, thus spreading the good word about keeping aquarium fish.

chapter 2

Taxonomic description of Indian Fishes

INTRODUCTION

There is enormous diversity in the morphology, habitats and biology of fish. Fish are heterogenous. They can be defined simply as cold-blooded vertebrates that possess gills, and limbs in the shape of fins.

There are approximately 21,723 species of living fish compared to extinct species numbering 21,450 (Nelson, 1984). Fish generally live in fresh or marine waters, but there are many in most categories which are *diadromous*, regularly living part of their lives in fresh water and partly in the seas. The Indian sub-continent, which includes India, Pakistan, Sri Lanka, Bangladesh, Nepal and Myanmar, so far possesses 930 described fish species.

This book deals only with fish which can be labelled as 'aquarium worthy'. Therefore, in the descriptions of various fish species, there are many families and orders which have been completely omitted. Many species from the omitted groups are beautiful and could be popular with aquarists, but little is known about these fish – however the quest is on to introduce these fish successfully to the aquaria, which could eventually lead to a second book on this fascinating subject.

Fish can be broadly classified into two categories:

* Class **Chondrichthyes**: These cartilaginous fishes have five gill openings in each side of the head. Fish in this group include sharks, rays and skates.
* Class **Osteichthyes**: These bony fishes, which have only one gill opening on each side of the head, comprise the rest of the fishes that are found.

The first class of cartilaginous fishes is totally omitted from this book and only aquarium-worthy species of the class of Bony Fishes are described here.

Table 2.1 General Classification of Indian Species of Class Osteichthyes, Subclass Actinopterygii, Subdivision Teleostei.

Order Osteoglossiformes

| Family | Notopteridae | Knife Fishes |
| Genus | *Notopterus* (Lacepede) | |

Order Elopiformes

Suborder	Elopoidei	
Family	Megalopidae	Tarpons
Genus	Megalops (Lacepede)	
Suborder	Albuldidei	

| Family | Albuldidae | Bone Fishes |
| Genus | Albula (Scopoli) | |

Order Anguilliformes

Family	Anguillidae	Eels
Genus	*Anguilla* (Schrank)	
Family	Moringuidae	Worm Eels
Genus	Moringua (Gray)	
Family	Muraenidae	Moray Eels
Genus	*Lycodontis* (McClelland)	
Genus	*Thyrsoidea* (Kaup)	
Family	Ophichthidae	Snake Eels
Subfamily	Ophichthidae	
Genus	*Bascanichthys* (Jordan and Davis)	
Genus	*Caecula* (Vahl)	
Genus	*Lamnostoma* (Kaup)	
Genus	*Pisodonophis* (Kaup)	
Family	Muraenesocidae	Pike Congers
Genus	*Congresox* (Gill)	
Genus	*Muraenesox* (McClelland)	

Order Clupeiformes

Family	Clupeidaie	Herrings, Sardines, Shads
Subfamily	Alosinae	Shads
Genus	*Gudusia* (Fowler)	
Genus	*Hilsa* (Regan)	
Subfamily	Dorosomatinae	Gizzard Shads
Genus	*Anodontosoma* (Bleeker)	
Genus	*Gonialosa* (Regan)	
Genus	*Nematolosa* (Regan)	
Subfamily	Pellonulinae	Freshwater Herrings
Genus	*Corica* (Hamilton-Buchanan)	
Genus	*Dayella* (Talwar and Whitehead)	
Genus	*Ehirava* (Deraniyagala)	
Family	Pristigasteridae	Ilishas, Pellonas
Genus	*Ilisha* (Richardson)	
Genus	*Opisthopterus* (Gill)	
Genus	*Pellona* (Valenciennes)	
Genus	*Raconda* (Gray)	

Family	Engraulididae	Anchovies
Genus	*Coilia* (Gray)	
Genus	*Setipinna* (Swainson)	
Genus	*Stolephorus* (Lacepede)	
Genus	*Thryssa* (Cuvier)	

INFRADIVISION EUTELEOSTEI

Order Gonorhynchiformes

Family	Chanidae	Milkfish
Genus	*Chanos* (Lacepede)	

Order Cypriniformes

Family	Cyprinidae	Carps and Minnows
Subfamily	Cyprininae	Barbs
Genus	Cirrhinus (Oken)	
Genus	*Capoeta* (Valenciennes)	
Genus	*Carassius* (Jarocki)	Introduced species
Genus	*Catla* (Valenciennes)	
Genus	*Chagunius* (Smith)	
Genus	*Ctenopharyngodon* (Steindachner)	
Genus	*Cyclocheilichthys* (Bleeker)	
Genus	*Cyprinion* (Heckel)	
Genus	Cyprinus (Linnaeus)	
Genus	*Gonoproktopterus* (Bleeker)	
Genus	*Hampala* (Bleeker)	
Genus	*Labeo* (Cuvier)	
Genus	*Labiobarbus* (Van Hasselt)	
Genus	*Mystacoleucus* (Gunther)	
Genus	*Neolissochilus* (Rainboth)	
Genus	*Oreichthys* (Smith)	
Genus	*Osteobrama* (Heckel)	
Genus	Osteocheilus (Gunther)	
Genus	*Osteochilichthys* (Hora)	
Genus	*Puntius* (Hamilton-Buchanan)	
Genus	*Rohtee* (Sykes)	
Genus	*Sawbwa* (Annandale)	
Genus	Saphiodonichthys (Vinciguerra)	
Genus	*Schismatorhynchos* (Bleeker)	
Genus	*Thynnichthys* (Bleeker)	
Genus	*Tinca* (Cuvier)	
Genus	*Tor* (Gray)	
Subfamily	Cultrinae	Hatchet Fish, Razorbellies
Genus	*Chela* (Hamilton-Buchanan)	
Genus	*Inlecyris* (Howes)	
Genus	*Salmostoma* (Swainson)	

Genus	Securicula (Hamilton-Buchanan)	
Subfamily	Leuciscinae	Silver Carp
Genus	*Hypophthalmichthys* (Bleeker)	Introduced species
Subfamily	Rasborinae	Carplets, Hill Trouts; Pencil Fish, Danios, Rasboras
Genus	*Amblypharyngodon* (Bleeker)	
Genus	*Aspidoparia* (Heckel)	
Genus	*Barilius* (Hamilton-Buchanan)	
Genus	*Bengala* (Gray)	
Genus	*Brachydanio* (Weber and de Beaufort)	
Genus	*Danio* (Hamilton-Buchanan)	
Genus	*Esomus* (Swainson)	
Genus	*Horadandia* (Deraniyagala)	
Genus	*Microrasbora* (Annadale)	
Genus	*Parluciosoma* (Howes)	
Genus	*Raiamas* (Jordan)	
Genus	*Rasbora* (Bleeker)	
Subfamily	Schizothracinae	Snow Trouts; Snow Minnows
Genus	*Diptychus* (Steindachner)	
Genus	*Gymnocypris* (Gunther)	
Genus	*Lepidopygopsis* (Raj)	
Genus	*Ptychobarbus* (Steindachner)	
Genus	*Schizocypris* (Regan)	
Genus	*Schizopygopsis* (Steindachner)	
Genus	*Schizothoraichthys* (Misra)	
Genus	*Schizothorax* (Heckel)	
Subfamily	Garrinae	Algaeaters
Genus	*Crossocheilus* (Kuhl et van Hasselt)	
Genus	*Garra* (Hamilton-Buchanan)	
Family	Parapsilorhynchidae	Sucker Fish
Genus	*Parapsilorhynchus* (Hora)	
Family	Psilorhynchidae	Torrent Fish
Genus	*Psilorhynchus* (McClelland)	
Family	Balitoridae	Loaches
Genus	*Balitora* (Gray)	
Genus	*Bhavania* (Hora)	
Genus	*Homaloptera* (Van Hasselt)	
Genus	*Travancoria* (Hora)	
Subfamily	Nemacheilinae	Cylindrical Loaches

Genus	*Aborichthys* (Chaudhuri)	
Genus	*Noemacheilus* (van Hasselt)	
Genus	*Noemachilicthys* (Day)	
Genus	*Acanthocobitis* (Peters)	
Genus	*Schistura*	
Genus	*Trilophysa* (Rendahl)	
Family	Cobitidae	Spined Loaches
Subfamily	Cobitinae	Blunt Faced Loaches
Genus	*Acantopsis* (Van Hasselt)	
Genus	*Enobarbichthys* (Whitley)	
Genus	*Lepidocephalus* (Bleeker)	
Genus	*Misgurnus* (Lacepede)	
Genus	*Neoeucirrhichthys* (Banarescu and Nalbant)	
Genus	*Pangio* (Acanthophthalmus) (Blyth)	
Genus	*Somileptes* (Hamilton-Buchanan)	
Subfamily	Botiinae	Point Faced Loaches
Genus	*Botia* (Gray)	

Order Siluriformes

Family	Bagridae	Bagrid Catfishes
Genus	*Aorichthys* (Wu)	
Genus	*Batasio* (Blyth)	
Genus	*Horabagrus* (Jayaram)	
Genus	*Mystus* (Scopoli)	
Genus	*Chandramara* (Jayaram)	
Genus	*Rita* (Bleeker)	
Family	Siluridae	Eurasian Catfishes
Genus	*Kryptopterus* (Bleeker)	
Genus	*Ompok* (Lacepede)	
Genus	*Pinniwallago* (Gupta, Jayaram & Hajela)	
Genus	*Siluris* (Linnaeus)	
Genus	*Wallago* (Bleeker)	
Family	Schilbeidae	Schilbid Catfishes
Subfamily	Ailiinae	Fountain Whiskered Catfishes
Genus	*Ailia* (Gray)	
Subfamily	Schilbeinae	Shark Catfishes
Genus	*Clupisoma* (Swainson)	
Genus	*Eutropiichthys* (Bleeker)	
Genus	*Neotropius* (Kulkarni)	
Genus	*Pseudeutropius* (Bleeker)	
Genus	*Proeutropiichthys* (Hora)	

Genus	*Silonia* (Swainson)	
Family	Pangasiidae	Tiger Sharks
Genus	*Pangasius* (Valenciennes)	
Family	Amblycipitidae	Scissors Tail Catfishes
Genus	*Amblyceps* (Blyth)	
Family	Akysidae	Stream Catfishes
Genus	*Akysis* (Bleeker)	
Family	Sisoridae	Whiptail Catfishes, Giant Catfishes
Genus	*Bagarius* (Bleeker)	
Genus	*Conta* (Hora)	
Genus	*Coraglanis* (Hora and Silas)	
Genus	*Erethistes* (Muller and Troschel)	
Genus	*Erethistoires* (Hora)	
Genus	*Euchiloganis* (Regan)	
Genus	*Exostoma* (Blyth)	
Genus	*Gagata* (Bleeker)	
Genus	*Glyposternum* (McClelland)	
Genus	*Glyptothorax* (Blyth)	
Genus	*Hara* (Blyth)	
Genus	*Laguvia* (Hora)	
Genus	*Myersglanis* (Hora and Silas)	
Genus	*Nangra* (Day)	
Genus	*Oreoglanis* (Smith)	
Genus	*Pseudechenesis* (Blyth)	
Genus	*Pseudolaguvia* (Misra)	
Genus	*Sisor* (Hamilton-Buchanan)	
Family	Clariidae	Air Breathing Catfishes
Genus	*Clarias* (Scopoli)	
Genus	*Horaglanis* (Menon)	
Family	Heteropneustidae	Stinging Catfishes
Genus	*Heteropneustes* (Muller)	
Family	Chacidae	Squarehead or Angler Catfishes
Genus	*Chaca* (Gray)	
Family	Olyridae	Fighting Catfishes
Genus	*Olyra* (McClelland)	
Family	Ariidae	Sea Catfishes

Genus	*Arius* (Valenciennes)	
Genus	*Batrachocephalus* (Bleeker)	
Genus	*Hemipimelodus* (Bleeker)	
Genus	*Ketengus* (Bleeker)	
Genus	*Osteogeneiosus* (Bleeker)	
Family	Plotosidae	Eel Tail Catfishes
Genus	*Plotosus* (Lacepede)	

Order Salmoniformes

Family	Salmonidae	Salmonids, Trouts
Genus	*Oncorhynchus* (Suckley)	
Genus	*Salmo* (Linnaeus)	
Genus	*Salvelinus* (Richardson)	

Order Aulopiformes

Family	Harpadontidae	Bombay Ducks
Genus	*Harpadon* (Le Sueur)	

Order Batrachoidiformes

Family	Batrachoididae	Toad Fishes
Genus	*Batrichthys* (Smith)	

Order Cyprinodontiformes

Suborder	Exocoetoidei	
Family	Hemiramphidae	Halfbeaks
Genus	*Dermogenys* (Van Hasselt)	
Genus	*Hyporhamphus* (Gill)	
Genus	*Zenarchopterus* (Gill)	
Family	*Belonidae*	Garfishes
Genus	*Strongylura* (Van Hasselt)	
Genus	*Xenentodon* (Regan)	
Suborder	Adrianichthyoidei	
Family	Oryziidae	Medakas or Ricefishes
Genus	*Oryzias* (Jordan and Snyder)	
Family	Horaichthyidae	Thready Killifishes
Genus	*Horaichthys* (Kulkarni)	
Suborder	Cyprinodontoidei	
Family	Aplocheilidae	Panchax
Genus	*Aplocheilus* (McClelland)	
Family	Cyprinodontidae	Killifishes
Genus	*Aphanius* (Nardo)	

Family	Poecilidae	Livebearers (introduced)
Genus	*Gambusia* (Poey)	
Genus	*Poecilia* (Bloch and Schneider)	

Order Indostomiformes

| Family | Indostomidae | Indostomids |
| Genus | *Indostomus* (Prashad and Mukerji) | |

Order Syngnathiformes

Family	Syngnathidae	Seahorses and Pipe Fish
Genus	*Hippichthys* (Bleeker)	
Genus	*Hippocampus* (Rafinesque)	
Genus	*Ichthyocampus* (Kaup)	
Genus	*Microphis* (Kaup)	

Order Synbranchiformes

Family	Synbranchidae	Swamp Eels
Genus	*Monopterus* (Lacepede)	
Genus	*Ophisternon* (McClelland)	

Order Scorpaeniformes

Family	Platycephalidae	Flatheads
Genus	*Grammoplites* (Fowler)	
Genus	*Platycephalus* (Bloch)	

Order Perciformes

Suborder	Percoidei	
Family	Centropomidae	Barramundis
Genus	*Lates* (Cuvier)	
Genus	*Psammoperca* (Richardson)	
Family	Ambassidae	Glassfishes
Genus	*Ambassis* (Cuvier)	
Genus	*Chanda* (Hamilton-Buchanan)	
Genus	*Parambassis* (Bleeker)	
Genus	*Pseudambassis* (Bleeker)	
Family	Serranidae	Groupers
Genus	*Epinephalus* (Bloch)	
Genus	*Promicrops* (Gill)	
Family	Teraponidae	Targetfishes
Genus	*Pelates* (Cuvier)	
Genus	*Terapon* (Cuvier)	
Family	Kuhliidae	Flagtails

Genus	*Kuhlia* (Gill)	
Family	Sillaginiidae	Whitings
Genus	*Sillaginopsis* (Gill)	
Genus	*Sillago* (Cuvier)	
Family	Carangidae	Kingfishes
Genus	*Carangoides* (Bleeker)	
Genus	*Caranx* (Lacepede)	
Genus	*Megalaspis* (Bleeker)	
Genus	*Scomberoides* (Lacepede)	
Family	Leiognathidae	Ponytails
Genus	*Gazza* (Ruppell)	
Genus	*Leiognathus* (Lacepede)	
Genus	*Secutor* (Gistel)	
Family	Lutjanidae	Snappers
Genus	*Lutjanus* (Bloch)	
Family	Lobotidae	Tripletails
Genus	*Datnioides* (Bleeker)	
Genus	*Lobotes* (Cuvier)	
Family	Gerreidae	Silver Biddies
Genus	*Gerreomorpha* (Alleyene and Mackay)	
Genus	*Gerres* (Cuvier)	
Family	Haemulidae	Grunters
Genus	*Pomadasys* (Lacepede)	
Family	Sparidae	Porgies
Genus	*Acanthopagrus* (Peters)	
Genus	*Crenidens* (Valenciennes)	
Genus	*Rhabdosargus* (Fowler)	
Family	Sciaenidae	Croakers
Genus	*Bahaba* (Herre)	
Genus	*Daysciaena* (Talwar)	
Genus	*Dendrophysa* (Trewavas)	
Genus	*Johnieops* (Mohan)	
Genus	*Johnius* (Bloch)	
Genus	*Macrospinosa* (Mohan)	
Genus	*Otolithoides* (Fowler)	
Genus	*Pama* (Fowler)	
Genus	*Panna* (Mohan)	

Genus	*Protonibea* (Trewavas)	
Genus	*Pterotolithus* (Fowler)	
Family	Mullidae	Goatfishes
Genus	*Upeneus* (Cuvier)	
Family	Monodactylidae	Finger Fishes
Genus	*Monodactylus* (Lacepede)	
Family	Toxotidae	Archerfishes
Genus	*Toxotes* (Cuvier)	
Family	Kyphosidae	Rudderfishes
Genus	*Kyphosus* (Lacepede)	
Family	Drepanidae	Sicklefishes
Genus	*Drepane* (Cuvier)	
Family	Scactophagidae	Scats
Genus	*Scatophagus* (Cuvier)	
Family	Nandidae	Leaffishes
Subfamily	Nandinae	True Leaffishes
Genus	*Nandus* (Valenciennes)	
Subfamily	Pristolepidinae	Sunfishes
Genus	*Pristolepsis* (Jerdon)	
Subfamily	Badinae	Dwarf Chameleon Fishes
Genus	*Badis* (Bleeker)	
Family	Cichlidae	Cichlids
Genus	*Etroplus* (Cuvier)	
Genus	*Oreochromis* (Gunther)Introduced species	
Suborder	Mugiloidei	
Family	Mugilidae	
Genus	*Liza* (Jordan and Swain)	
Genus	*Mugil* (Linnaeus)	
Genus	*Rhinomugil* (Gill)	
Genus	*Sicamugil* (Fowler)	
Genus	*Valamugil* (Smith)	
Suborder	Sphyraenoidei	
Family	Sphyraenidae	Barracudas
Genus	*Sphyraena* (Rose)	
Suborder	Polynemoidei	

Family	Polynemidae	Threadfins
Genus	*Eleutheronema* (Bleeker)	
Genus	*Polydactylus* (Lacepede)	
Genus	*Polynemus* (Linnaeus)	
Suborder	Blennioidei	
Family	Blennidae	Blennies
Genus	*Omobranchus* (Ehrenberg)	
Suborder	Callionymoidei	
Family	Callionymidae	Dragonets
Genus	*Callionymus* (Linnaeus)	
Genus	*Eleutherochir* (Bleeker)	
Suborder	Gobioidei	
Family	Gobiidae	Gobies
Subfamily	Gobiinae	True Gobies
Genus	*Acentrogobius* (Bleeker)	
Genus	*Awaous* (Valenciennes)	
Genus	*Bathygobius* (Bleeker)	
Genus	*Brachygobius* (Bleeker)	
Genus	*Callogobius* (Bleeker)	
Genus	*Chiramenu* (Rao)	
Genus	*Cryptocentrus* (Valenciennes)	
Genus	*Favonigobius* (Whitley)	
Genus	*Glossogobius* (Gill)	
Genus	*Goniopsis* (Steindachner)	
Genus	*Mahidolia* (Smith)	
Genus	*Oligolepis* (Bleeker)	
Genus	*Oxyurichthys* (Bleeker)	
Genus	*Parachaeturichthys* (Bleeker)	
Genus	*Paroxyurichthys* (Bleeker)	
Genus	*Silhouettea* (Smith)	
Genus	*Stenogobius* (Bleeker)	
Genus	*Stigmatogobius* (Bleeker)	
Subfamily	Apocrypteinae	Elongated Gobies
Genus	*Apocryptes* (Valenciennes)	
Genus	*Apocryptes* (Bleeker)	
Genus	*Boleophthalmus* (Valenciennes)	
Genus	*Oxuderces* (Eydoux and Souleyet)	
Genus	*Parapocryptes* (Bleeker)	
Genus	*Pseudapocryptes* (Bleeker)	
Genus	*Scartelaos* (Swainson)	
Subfamily	Periophthalminae	Mudskippers

Genus	*Periophthalmodon* (Bleeker)	
Genus	*Periophthalmus* (Bloch and Schneider)	
Subfamily	Sicydiaphiinae	Neon Gobies
Genus	*Gobiopterus* (Bleeker)	
Genus	*Sicyopterus* (Gill)	
Family	Eleotrididae	Sleepers
Genus	*Butis* (Bleeker)	
Genus	*Eleotris* (Schneider)	
Genus	*Incara* (Rao)	
Genus	*Odonteleotris* (Gill)	
Genus	*Ophieleotris* (Aurich)	
Genus	*Ophiocara* (Gill)	
Family	Gobiodidae	Eel-like Gobies
Genus	*Brachyamblyopus* (Bleeker)	
Genus	*Odontamblyopus* (Bleeker)	
Genus	*Taenioides* (Lacepede)	
Family	Trypauchenidae	Burrowing Gobies
Genus	*Ctenotrypauchen* (Steindachner)	
Genus	*Trypauchen* (Valenciennes)	
Family	Kraemeriidae	Sand Gobies
Genus	*Kraemericus* (Schultz)	
Suborder	Kurtidei	
Family	Kurtiidae	Nurseryfishes
Genus	*Kurtus* (Bloch)	
Suborder	Scombroidei	
Family	Trichiuridae	Ribbonfishes
Genus	*Lepturacanthus* (Fowler)	
Genus	*Trichiurus* (Linnaeus)	
Suborder	Anabantoidei	
Family	Anabantidae	Climbing Perches
Genus	*Anabas* (Cuvier and Cloquet)	
Family	Belontiidae	Gouramies
Subfamily	Belontiinae	Combtail Gouramies
Genus	*Belontia* (Myers)	
Subfamily	Macropodinae	Paradise Fishes
Genus	*Ctenops* (McClelland)	

Genus	*Pharasomenus*	
Genus	*Malpulutta* (Deraniyagala)	
Subfamily	Trichogasterinae	True Gouramies
Genus	*Colisa* (Cuvier)	
Genus	*Parasphaerichthys* (Prashad and Mukerji)	
Genus	*Trichogaster* (Schneider)	
Family	Helostomatidae	Kissing Gouramies (introduced)
Genus	*Helostoma* (Cuvier)	
Family	Osphronemidae (Lacepede)	Giant Gouramies (introduced)
Genus	*Osphronemus* (Lacepede)	
Suborder	Channoidei	
Family	Channidae	Snakeheads
Genus	*Channa* (Scopoli)	

Order Mastacembeliformes

Suborder	Mastacembeloidei	
Family	Mastacembelidae	Spiny Eels
Genus	*Macrognathus* (Lacepede)	
Genus	Mastacembelus (Scopoli)	
Family	Chaudhuriidae	Spineless Eels
Genus	*Chaudhuria* (Annandale)	
Family	Pilaiidae	Subcylindrical Eels
Pillaia		
Garo		

Order Pleuronectiformes

Family	Bothidae	Left Eye Flounders
Subfamily	Paralichthyinae	
Genus	*Pseudorhombus* (Bleeker)	
Suborder	Soleoidei	
Family	Cynoglossidae	Tongue Fishes
Genus	*Cynoglossus* (Hamilton-Buchanan)	
Genus	*Paraplagusia* (Bleeker)	
Family	Soleidae	Soles
Genus	*Euryglossa* (Kaup)	
Genus	*Synaptura* (Cantor)	

Order Tetraondontiformes

Suborder	Balistoidei	
Family	Triacanthidae	Tripod Fishes
Genus	Triacanthus (Cuvier)	
Suborder	Tetraondontoidei	
Family	Tetraondontidae	Puffer Fishes
Genus	*Arothron* (Muller)	
Genus	*Chelonodon* (Muller)	
Genus	*Lagocephalus* (Swainson)	
Genus	*Takifugu* (Abe)	
Genus	*Tetraodon* (Linnaeus)	
Genus	*Monotretus* (Hora and Nair)	
Genus	*Xenopterus* (Bibron)	

The Teesta.

TELEOSTS

The subclass *Actinopterygii* includes the advanced Bony Fishes. The teleosts, or modern bony fishes, are the largest and most diverse group. Comprising about 20800 species (Nelson, 1984), the teleosts have radiated into every aquatic niche of our planet, from high mountain streams to the greatest depths of the ocean, from deep caves and tropical swamps to the polar seas. Teleosts are of great importance economically and as members of the aquatic ecosystems of the world. The most common food fishes (including carps, sardines, catfishes, shads and soles) are all teleosts.

Featherbacks: Family Notopteridae

In India there are two species of this family, which are predominantly tropical freshwater fishes of extraordinarily diverse body form and size. Featherbacks are easily identified by the very long anal fin which begins just behind the head and extends along the undersurface of the body to the tip of the anal fin. The tailfin as such is not evident. In the centre of the back is a small slender dorsal fin from which these fish derive the name 'Featherback'.

In aquarists' jargon, these fish are popularly known as 'Knife Fishes'. There is a great difference in the size of the two known species found in India. The much larger, if not giant, Clown Knife prefers weedy reaches of great rivers and is found throughout almost the whole of North and North-eastern India. The much smaller Black Knife Fish is found throughout India in stagnant backwaters. These are perfect for display in public aquaria. They *seem* very peaceful, and are very graceful in their movements – but they are very predatory by nature and will consume smaller fish with wild abandon as they have enormous appetites. Nocturnal by nature, a dimly-lit tank with some large rocks suit these fish best.

Freshwater Eels: Family Anguillidae

These eels live in a variety of freshwater habitats, such as streams, rivers, ponds and lakes and are *catadromous*, which means that they descend periodically for spawning to the lower parts of the river or the sea. Freshwater eels are an important source of food in many parts of the world and several species are cultured in Asia. These eels are yet to be farmed in India, and those caught in the fishermen's nets seldom reach the markets in the bigger cities, so one does not often come across these exotic but common fish. Some species attain a length of 180cm and weigh up to 20 kilograms. They are highly valued as food and many people believe they are good for people suffering from blood ailments.

Very rarely exported by the aquarium trade are the Brown Snake Eel and the Bicolor Snake Eel. The young readily take live foods; the larger specimens are reluctant to take food at first but are able to survive long periods of time without eating. These are shy fish which do best in dimly-lit aquaria containing hollow logs or pipes where they can hide lengthwise without having to coil up in a smaller shelter. Some of these eels have been known to become quite tame and lift their heads out of the water to investigate their owner's fingers for any sign of food or simply out of curiosity.

Worm Eels: Family Mornguidae

The only species of these relatively less-known eels is the Pink Worm Eel which has been kept in aquaria for some time now. These bright pink eels, averaging 18cm, have beady, jet-black eyes. They are burrowing fish and prefer to stay submerged with their snouts pointing out, so they only survive in aquaria with some form of sandy substrate.

Moray Eels: Family Moringuidae

The Spotted Moray Eel is the freshwater aquarist's dream come true. Here the aquarist can get a reasonably attractive dwarf moray. It looks just like the 'real thing', can live comfortably in fresh water and even eats live Tubifex worms. This is the only one of the three species found in India which so far has been kept successfully in the freshwater aquaria by the amateur hobbyist.

Olive Eels: Family Ophichthidae

Out of the five species of this family found in the Indian region, only one species is commonly encountered within the aquarium trade – the Olive Eel. It is not a particularly attractive fish, but it is amazing to see it move around the aquaria.

Carps and Minnows: Family Cyprinidae

This important family of freshwater fishes is distributed throughout Africa (except Madagascar), Asia, Europe and North America. It is a very large and dominant group of primary freshwater fishes in most of the areas within its distribution and is of considerable economic significance in India. This is the largest family of fishes, comprising about 194 genera and 2070 species (Nelson, 1984) and includes Goldfish, Minnows, Barbs, Rasboras and Danios.

Barbs: Subfamily Cyprinae

This subfamily consists of the largest group of freshwater fishes which are economically important as food fishes as well as aquarium fishes. This subfamily contains the great bulk of the cyprinoid fishes of India and adjacent countries. Several hundred species are known from Europe, Africa and Asia, but by far the most popular in the aquarium trade come from the regions of India and Malaysia. There are approximately 25 genera in the Indian region itself.

The formation of the mouth parts of this subfamily is very diverse, but the three main types can be distinguished easily (Talwar and Jhingran):

1. In the most simple type, the mouth is terminal or subinferior and more or less protractile; lips are thin or thick, crenulated or papillated ('lip' is understood to mean a more-or-less developed fold of skin which is fairly distinctly separated from the covering of the jaws).

2. In the second type the mouth is conspicuously inferior, burrowed by thick and continuous lips, which may be fringed or papillated. The upper lip is partly covered or bordered by a pendulous rostral fold of the skin of the ventral surface of the rostrum (as is evident in the genus *Labeo*).

3. In the third type the mouth is inferior, wide and has an exposed cornified, mandibular cutting edge which is not covered by a thick labial fold (fleshy lip). Such a mouth is referred to as 'sector mouth' (Howes, 1980) and is found in the genera *Cyprinion* and *Capoeta*. In many Cyprininae, the lower lip is separated from the skin of the isthmus by a complete postlabial groove which is continued round the corners of the mouth. This groove may be interrupted in the middle so that there are separate grooves, one behind each lateral part of the lower lip, as is seen in *Osteochilus* and *Labiobarbus*.

There follows brief descriptions on various genera of this vast subfamily, each of which consists of one or more Indian species which have been used for aquaria, or which could have good potential as interesting fish to be kept successfully as pets.

Genus Catla: Popularly called Thicklips, this fish is a much-favoured delicacy among the people of Eastern India. It grows quite large, up to 120cm under favourable environmental conditions. This riverine species is non-predatory and its feeding is restricted to the surface and midwaters. Being a commercially-important fish, it has been introduced into almost all parts of India and is reared in tanks and ponds. These are very hardy fish which, when young, withstand transportation well over long distances involving considerable time. It is a good fish for pond or tank angling as it fights well.

Five hybrids have been produced in India, namely:
* male *Catla* x female *L.Rohita*;
* male *Catla* x female *L.Calbasu*;
* male *Catla* x female *C.Mrigala*;
* male *L.Rohita* x female *Catla*;
* male L *Fimbriatus* x female *Catla*.

In 1962, one pair of *Catla–L. Rohita* hybrids was injected with a pituitary hormone and induced to spawn, which resulted in the successful production of a second generation of the hybrid. In 1960, several hundred golden-coloured *Catla* were obtained from one induced-bred specimen and, when the coloured *Catla* were interbred, all the progeny were found to be coloured (Jhingran and Pullin, 1985). This unique carp has often been confused with an allied genus, *Catlocarpio*, which occurs in Thailand, as there is an extraordinary likeness between the two species, especially in the enormous head.

Thicklips which have been circulated in the aquaruam trade are purely wild fish, collected after the monsoon from the mighty Brahmaputra river of Assam, North-eastern India.

Genus Cirrhinus: White Carps The Cirrhinid fishes of India form a fairly distinct group which ranges in the southern part of East Asia and in Continental South Asia (the Indian Subcontinent, Myanmar and basins of the Menam and Mekong rivers), being absent from the Malaysian Peninsula and the Indonesian Islands. This group apparently resembles Labeos, but differences are seen in the lower lip which is closely attached to the lower jaw, and in the absence of inner labial folds. There are approximately ten species with five in India which can be assigned to subgenera Cirrhinus and Henicorhynchus. Noteworthy among these is the Mrigal which is a fine fish of elegant appearance. It is a major carp of India and quite a game fish. In its natural waters - two of the most important rivers in India, Ganga and Yamuna - Mrigal is known to attain a length of 99cm and a weight of 12.7kg. In natural, open waters it breeds during the south-west monsoon in shallow pockets in marginal areas, and in bundhs. Mrigal is a detritus eater with a narrow range in food variety. It is a bottom feeder subsisting mainly on decayed vegetation.

Genus Gonoproktopterus: These are giant barbs which attain average lengths of 60cm and more. Members of this genus are found only in Peninsular India in large upland rivers. The taxonomy and systematics of the various species are poorly known. Six species are recognised. The best known of these exotic barbs is the very rare and seldom seen Red Tailed Silver Shark which can attain a length of 1.2m. It lives and breeds in hilly terrain but comes down to tidal reaches for feeding. Breeding occurs in small streams with sandy, weedy bottoms. Males mature when they are 10cm long and females at 15cm. Adults in the wild feed mostly on algae and, occasionally, insect larvae.

Genus Labeo: Sharks The famous and fantastically coloured Red Tail Black Shark (*Labeo bicolor*) of Thailand was the first fish of this large group of predominantly excellent food fish to be sold by aquarium retailers as 'sharks', which boosted sales to astronomical heights. Thereafter, nearly all the species of Labeo introduced into the aquarium trade were popularly known as 'sharks'. Incidentally, according to recent nomenclatural rectification, *Labeo bicolor* is now known as *Epalzeorhynchus bicolor*. This genus is widely distributed in South and South-east Asia and Africa. It is extremely well represented in India where some of the species reach a length of 1.5m. There are numerous species, 31 in the Indian region. The All Black Shark (*Labeo calbasu*) has an almost identical cousin in Thailand, *Morulius chrysophekadion*, and was until recently the only Labeo from India to be utilised in the aquarium trade. Now, the strikingly beautiful Red Gilled Violet Shark (*Labeo boga*) is emerging as a hot favourite with aquarists the world over. Fortunately, these fish do not inherit the pugnacious and sometimes intolerant moods that most Labeos exhibit in aquaria to other fish and, frequently, to their own species.

Genus Oreichthys: Hi-Fin Barbs Only two known species exist of Oreichthys. One, *O. Cosuatis*, has been known to science since 1822, but the other (*O. Umangii*) was overlooked until recently described by the author (in press). The most remarkable feature of this genus appears to be the presence of numerous fine, parallel sensory folds on the sides of the head. This feature is shared with the fishes of the genus Cyclochilichthys, but differs in that the last simple dorsal fin ray is non-osseus and non-denticulated.

Genus Osteobrama: Diamond Barbs This genus is Oriental and is restricted to Pakistan, India, Bangladesh, Myanmar and Yunnan (China). Several species exist, seven in the Indian region. At first glance, these could be mistaken for large Glass Fishes of the genus *Ambassis*.

Genus Puntius: True Barbs This great group is a specific group of Cyprinid fishes and is Oriental. The Puntius fishes are commonly called Barbs and are widely distributed in Southeast Asia. Intraspecific variability of colour pattern coupled, on occasion, with similar intraspecific morphometric and meristic characters, have made it very difficult to distinguish between species. Many species are known only by typical specimens and have not been recorded since their original discovery. The entire range of about 70 species so far known from the Indian region has been brought down to 53.

Until recent years these fishes were placed in the genus *Barbus Cuvier*. The use of the generic name Barbus is limited to the African and European species with *Barbus barbus* (L.) as the type. According to Chu (1935), many ichthyologists have made a serious mistake by adopting this generic name for the numerous Asiatic species, which differ widely from each other and from *Barbus barbus* (L.).

There is hardly a freshwater body in the Indian region where one does not encounter some Puntius species. Though most of them do not grow very large, they compensate by their abundance, and thus are economically important. Some small Puntius species are typically a plain silvery colour throughout whereas others have variable patterns of spots and/or stripes.

The most popular Puntius species from India are the Golden Dwarf Barb and Melon Barb. These fish show marked variations in colour depending upon the areas they come from. The former, also known as the Gelius Barb, is found throughout the North-eastern and Eastern parts of India. Both Gelius Barb and Melon Barb are basically golden yellow in colour but ruby-red fish of each species are found in certain areas, for example, red Gelius Barb are found in Muzaffarpur in Bihar. The Melon Barb is found from Goa in Western India south to Thiruvantapuram in Kerala. Males of a dazzling metallic ruby red are found in a single area of Karnataka near Bangalore. However, the rest of the Puntius species in India do not have much variation in colour or pattern. One fish worth mentioning is the simply brilliant Red Line Torpedo Fish. This species is found in the rockpools at the feet of waterfalls and, surprisingly, they never venture out of their rockpools into the on-flowing rivers. They resemble a Rasbora more than a Puntius. Until recently they were only known by the specimens collected by Francis Day in 1865, which are in the collection of the Zoological Survey of India. In 1996, the author (Rao) together with Mr Rohan Pethyagoda of the Sri Lankan Wildlife Heritage Trust, collected this fish from a single pool at the base of a waterfall at a site in Kerala. The author exhibited it at the 1997 Aquarama New Species Wild Caught Category, where it won the third prize.

Two other barbs, the Narayan's Barb and the Red Finned Barb, are fantastic in colour. The former is found near Mumbai in Western India and the latter was discovered by the author near Mangalore, Southwest India.

Genus Schismatorhynchos: Nukta Single genus, single species. The Double Mouth Tor is a Labeo-like fish with its snout projecting over the mouth, divided by a deep groove to a thick pronounced upper and a prominent lower part. Both parts are studded with large pores and tubercles which gives this fish the appearance of having a 'double mouth'.

Genus Tor: Mahseer Fish These Barbels (or Mahseers) are medium to large in size and are distributed from the Indus river basin to Borneo. They are among the most important cyprinid fishes of South and Southeast Asia. In India, along with Neolissochilus, they constitute the most important of the game fishes. They primarily inhabit the streams, rivers and lakes of the montane and submontane regions. There are several species, seven in India.

Subfamily: Cultrinae

The members of this subfamily are distributed in southeast Asia and China. This group of fishes may be distinguished by the greatly compressed body with a soft ventral keel which, in some species, extends the whole length of the abdomen. Of the 21 genera, four are in India.

Genus Chela: Hatchet Fishes These hatchet fishes, or 'oriental white minnows' are widely distributed in southeast Asia (inclusive of the islands) and are small (less than 7.5cm standard length) fishes. On a casual inspection, they are somewhat suggestive of the *Danio* and *Esomus* genera but are distinguished from the latter by the short dorsal fin and by the partly sharply-keeled edge to the belly. The fishes of this genus are shoaling and inhabit the upper water layers of streams, tanks, and ponds. The shape of the mouth and the deep body are adaptations associated with specialised surface or aerial feeding habits. When alive the fishes are more or less transparent. Six species are recognised at this time, four in India. The Burjor's Brilliance and the Malabar Hatchet are the colourful beauties of the four.

Genus Salmostoma: Razorbelly This interesting genus is made up of silver, elongated fishes of which there are 15 species, all in the Indian region. Worth mentioning is the Long Jawed Streak and the Silver Streak. The former reaches a length of 18cm and usually inhabits slow-running streams. It is a surface feeder and is regarded as a useful larvivorous fish. The sexes can be distinguished only by the female's greater girth. The Silver Streak attains a length of 12cm and inhabits streams, ponds and flooded fields.

Subfamily: Leuciscinae (Hypophthalmichthyinae)

Genus Hypophthalmichthys: Essentially this is a food fish, originally introduced from Amur and China into Taiwan, Thailand, Japan, Sri Lanka, India, Europe and North America. Of the three species, two were introduced into India.

Subfamily Rasborinae

This subfamily is well represented by both genera and species in the freshwaters of India and adjacent countries, and various of the species may be found in abundance.

Genus Amblypharyngodon: Carplets This Oriental genus inhabits the Indus plain and adjoining hilly areas (Pakistan), and also the plains and the adjoining areas of India, Bangladesh and Myanmar. The Brass Fish is popular among aquarists.

Genus Barilius: Hill Trouts The Barilins are for the most part fishes of hill or mountain streams although some species inhabit lowland water. The genus now includes only those species occuring in India, Nepal, Bangladesh, Sri Lanka, Myanmar and Thailand. Of the 27 species, 17 are found in the Indian region. The most striking is the majestic Blue Dotted Hill Trout, found in the Western Ghats of Kerala, Southwest India. This species attains a length of 15cm. The very rare Milk Fish found in Central India is almost heavenly with its silvery, milky appearance.

Genus Brachydanio: Dwarf Danios The fishes of this genus are small, slim, attractively coloured and active. They inhabit small water bodies and are commonest in mountain rivulets. This group is reported to have non-adhesive eggs and, when spawning, must be handled differently from other Danio groups. Of the several species, eight are in the Indian region.

Genus Danio: Danios This genus is indigenous to the Oriental region. These small, gorgeously-coloured, active fishes, which do not grow more than 11cm, are usually found in great abundance in small water courses such as pools, in rice fields, ditches in the beds of hillstreams, mountain rivulets and rivers. The name of this genus is derived from the Bengali word 'dhani' (belonging to dhan = paddy (rice or grain), which all the allied species are called by the Bengalis. The name may refer to their small size or to their being found in inundated paddy fields at the edges of rivers and lakes in grassy jungles. In this habitat their coloured stripes, loops and dashes are of great importance to these small fishes. There are several species, with 11 in the Indian region. Mention must be made of the exotic Moustached Danio, which won the second prize at Aquarama '95. This species of Danio has the longest two pairs of barbels, which enables the species to be identified from others in this genus. The Turquoise Danio, too, is a splendidly easy to keep fish.

Genus Esomus: Flying Barbs These small fish inhabit the shallow waters of small freshwaters – ponds, tanks, pools, paddy-fields and ditches where they breed freely. They prefer areas with profuse vegetation. These fishes have larvicidal value and are also used as aquarium pets. They are easily recognised by a pair of very long, slender maxillary barbels. Of the eight species, five are in the Indian region.

Genus Horadandia: Glowlight Carplet This is a monotypic genus. This is one of the smallest fishes found in India, rarely exceeding 1cm. They inhabit weedy freshwater ponds of the coastal plains. These dainty little fishes were thought to be found only in Sri Lanka but, during one of his extensive surveys in 1996, the author (Rao) found millions in a particular area in Kerala, where they co-existed with Panchax, Barbs and Dwarf Puffers. These are very peaceful and hardy fish.

Genus Parluciosoma: Slender Rasboras Cyprinids of this genus are small fishes inhabiting a rich variety of habitats in the lower reaches of mountain streams in Pakistan, India and Southeast Asia. They tend to be midwater dwellers. There are approximately nine species, and two of the giants of this group are found in India.

Genus Rasbora: Fish of this genus are tiny, elegant fishes (from 15–150mm standard length), inhabiting a rich variety of habitats from lakes to lower reaches of mountain streams and require study, attention and care. Some are in danger of becoming extinct. Some 50 valid species are presently recognised, all native to Southeast Asia, with four found in the Indian region. Mention must be made of the striking Yellow Tail Black Tip. Indian icthyologists believed that this fish inhabited only the Gangetic and Brahmaputra river provinces, but the author has collected them from the Tunghabhadra river in Karnataka, South India.

Subfamily Garrinae: Algaeaters
Genus Crossocheilus: This genus is Oriental, with two in the Indian region, but extends into Afghanistan and Iran. The fishes of this genus are small, growing to about 12.4cm. The World's Best Algaeater is nothing much to look at, being almost boring, but it is an excellent algae and refuse eater and is very sociable.

Genus Garra: This genus is widely represented in Asia and Africa. The fishes of this genus are adapted to life in swift-flowing mountain streams where they maintain their position in the strong currents by means of a small sucking disc on the lower lip. In addition, the fish presses its body firmly against the bottom and its large paired fins further increase the contact surface with the substratum. By virtue of these adaptations, these fishes are able to live even in rapids. The air-bladder is reduced to lessen buoyancy and the proboscis and tubercles help to lessen the velocity and impact of the rushing torrents suffered by these fishes. Food is mainly the algal felts on stones. However, in the aquaria they are not fussy eaters and will readily consume whatever is offered. Of the 35 species, 19 are in the Indian region. The Rhinocerous Algaeater is one fish to look out for.

Family Psilorhynchidae

Fishes of this family are known to occur primarily in the Gangetic river drainage of India. This family comprises a single genus of small hillstream fishes.

The raging Teesta River at the base of the Himalayas.

Genus Psilorhynchus: The five species of these freshwater fishes inhabit the mountain streams of India, Bangladesh, Nepal and Myanmar. These are small fishes, averaging maximum lengths of 8cm. Notable amongst this group are the Banded Torrent Fish and the Checkered Torrent Fish.
Family Balitoridae: Loaches

Subfamily Balitorinae: Hillstream Loaches

The Balitorids are small freshwater fishes extensively distributed in the hills of Southeastern Asia.

In India, they are found in the hills of Meghalaya and along the Eastern Himalayas as far as the Teesta and Kosi river drainages on the one hand, and the Western Ghats of Peninsular India on the other. They generally have rounded heads and streamlined bodies, and have adapted to life on the bottom of very swift mountain streams. Their shape and structure, particularly that of the fins, have adapted to the peculiarly harsh conditons of the environment. Their paired fins act as adhesive organs: the fish has developed a large sucking disc on its underside, the margins of which are formed by the pectoral and pelvic fins which extend laterally from the body, thus helping to provide a cup-like undersurface. These fishes build up a semi-vacuum between the substrate and the underside of their bodies by pumping their pectoral fins which removes the water from under the body. The maximum length is about 12cm. These fishes do well in aquaria but are not popular because of their drab appearance. There are approximately 28 genera containing about 120 species, and nine species in four genera are found in the Indian region.

Genus Homaloptera: Sucker Loaches This is the most numerous genus of the Homalopterid fishes and is represented in India only in the Western Ghats in Peninsular India. The genus is otherwise known from the Indo-Australian Archipelago and the Southeastern Asiatic mainland, being especially well represented in Java, Sumatra and Borneo. Four species are found in India, foremost being the Zig Zag Sucker Loach.

Genus Travancoria: Sucker Loaches

Only two species are found in India; the Angel Hillstream Sucker Loach was discovered very recently in Kerala and grows to about 12cm in length. This is not a very hardy species.

Subfamily Nemacheilinae: Cylindrical Loaches

This subfamily is widely distributed in the Oriental and Holarctic regions (except in North America). It comprises the loaches which are found mainly in montane and submontane regions rather than in the plains. They live among the pebbles at the bottom of shallow, clear and swift streams. This subfamily contains a large number of species in the genus *Nemacheilus*, and there are endless species waiting to be discovered.

Genus Aboricthys: Wedge Tail Loaches The fishes of the genus *Aborichthys* are adapted for life in torrential streams and are confined to northeastern India and Myanmar. Five species exist, all in India, the latest being the Sidewinder Loach, discovered by the author near Tura in the Garo Hills of Meghalaya.

Genus Nemacheilus: This genus consists of a group of species which are remarkably similar in their general morphology. Because they lack the usual spines, scutes and various other processes and peculiarities of structure, the species of *Nemacheilus* are often the most difficult to tell apart. Environmental conditions tend to produce similar characteristics and it is probable that the great resemblance between the various species are due to a similarity in their environment. The animals that inhabit such habitats have to adjust themselves constantly to any fluctuation in the microclimate or ecological niche. In these circumstances, their true systematic position becomes a matter of great difficulty. This is what has happened in *Nemacheilus*. The body has become more and more cylindrical, with the fins becoming smaller and more compact to facilitate the fish being amongst pebbles and shingles in swift-running waters. Over 450 species are described under this generic name. These species are quite diverse, and form several recognisable groups or subgenera. They inhabit the hillstreams of India and are restricted to South China, Southeast Asia, Baluchistan, Western Iran, South Anatolia and Lake Tsana in Northeast Africa. There are about

200 species, 63 in the Indian region. The most beautiful of these species are the Fascinating Loach, the Zodiac Loach and the newly-discovered Black Panther Loach. Notable subgenera of this group are *Noemachilicthys, Acanthocobitis* and *Schistura*.

Family Cobitidae: Spined Loaches

This family is distributed in Eurasia and Northern Africa, but the greatest diversity is in Southern Asia. They are bottom dwellers, mostly of small sizes (up to 30cm) and are found mainly in streams, rivers and lakes of hilly areas. The two sub-families are both in India.

Subfamily Cobitinae: Blunt Faced Loaches
Thirteen genera, seven in the Indian region.

Genus Lepidocephalus: Air Breathing Loaches The lepidocephalids are small fishes found mostly in swift streams but also in swamps and lakes. They appear to prefer a sandy or fine gravel bottom into which they are able to burrow and quickly disappear if alarmed or frightened. The spinous first pectoral ray helps with the 'digging in'. There are several species in two subgenera with seven species found in India. The Tail Spot Loach is a new entrant into the aquarium trade.

Genus Pangio: Snake Loaches These fishes are popularly called Coolie Loaches and are quite popular with aquarists. They range from Indonesia through Vietnam to India. These fishes inhabit standing or slowflowing waters. Of the several species, two are found in India.

Genus Somileptes: Jaguar Loach Also known as the Moose Faced Loach, this is a very odd-looking fish. It attains a length of 10cm and inhabits muddy hill streams. It is a very fussy eater in aquaria. This fish is quite rare in its range and is not a very hardy species.

Subfamily Botiinae: Point Faced Loaches
There are two genera, one of which is found in the Indian region.

Genus Botia These Loaches have slightly pointed snouts and live in the bottom of rapidly running water, mostly in upland areas. As a result of their environment, the Loach's gas bladder has adapted to help the fish survive.They have a large bifid suborbital spine which can be erected and which they use primarily for sifting the sand for blood and other worms and also as a defence mechanism to ward off attempts by predator fish. There are 22 species belong to three subgenera, of which nine species belonging to two subgenera are found in India. The genus is found from South China to Sumatra and South Borneo to the Indus river drainage. The Y-Loach or Tiger Loach and the Striped Loach are the most popular of the Indian Loaches.

ORDER SILURIFORMES: CATFISHES

The majority of Catfishes are easy to identify because their barbels extend from each side of the upper jaw; some also have them on the lower jaw. The major differences from other families of Ostariophysans are internal, but there are not many Catfishes which are not immediately recognisable as such as all but a few obscure ones have barbels. In many areas catfishes are popular sporting fish and a valued food item. These fishes are very numerous in the Indian sub-region and range in size from 5cm to 3m. The great majority of the species live only in freshwater, although some can invade brackish and sea water.

Several species of Catfishes are known to be venomous. They can inflict severe wounds with their spines (primarily those on the pectoral fin) and inject a poison produced by glandular cells in the epidermal tissue covering the spines. The classification of Catfishes is not settled and disagreement exists on the interrelationships of the families. The families of the Siluriformes known from the Indian region are arranged according to Nelson (1984).

Family Bagridae: Bagrid Catfishes

This family is widely distributed in Asia and Africa. They are mainly freshwater but at least one species, the Shadow Catfish, is partly marine. These grow very large and thus are important as food fish. There are 27 genera of which six are found in the Indian region. The magnificent Golden Redtailed Imperial Catfish, the Golden Headstander Catfish and the Velvet Catfish are the most attractive members of this group.

A large Shovelnose Catfish in a dinghy at Dibru River, Assam

Genus Aorichthys: Shovelmouth Catfishes This genus is widely distributed in the Oriental region and the two species are both found in the Indian region. These are giant Catfishes, commonly found in all the major rivers of India. They are unique because they build a nest where their eggs can hatch and the young ones shelter from predators.

Genus Batasio: Shark Catfishes: This genus is endemic to Southeast Asia; there are three species, all of which are found in the Indian region. These fish do not exceed 10cm in length. Interesting among these is the Translucent Shark Catfish.

Genus Horabagrus: Imperial Catfishes: Only two species are known: the Golden Redtailed Imperial Catfish and the recently-discovered White Collared Imperial Catfish. These spectacular fish are found in the southern state of Kerala. They attain a length of 45cm.

Genus Mystus: Mystus Catfishes Many of the species were once classified under the generic name *Macrones*. However, as certain differences were noted, they were put under *Mystus* (Dumeril, 1856) to which approximately 30 relatively generalised Asian Bagrid species are assigned, 19 of which are found in India. The most popular is the Zebra or Pyjama Striped Catfish.

Genus Chandramara: Hovering Catfishes Also known as the Asian Cory, this an extremely unusual small catfish which attains a length of 5cm. It is quite rare, being found only in the eastern and northeastern part of India.

Genus Rita: Whale Catfishes This genus is endemic to the Oriental region and is represented in the Indian area by four species. The southern limit in India is the river Krishna. However, it is common in the larger rivers of northern India. The bodies are rather short and compressed with large, depressed heads.

Family Siluridae: Eurasian Catfishes

The Eurasian Silurids is one of the most distinctive and well defined families of catfishes. These catfishes are freshwater inhabitants and are chiefly Asiatic in distribution. Aquarists are familiar with the Silurids through the popular Glass Catfish found in the Malayan–Indonesian region. There are 10 genera, five in the Indian region.

Genus Ompok: Butter Catfishes This genus is widely distributed in the Oriental region. There are seven species, four of which are found in India. The Gulper Cat Fish is a very interesting fish to keep as, true to its name, it gulps everything in sight!

Genus Wallago: Killer Catfishes Wallago comprises large Silurids, distinguished from all other genera in Southeast Asia by having a relatively large dorsal fin. It is widely distributed in the Oriental region as far as Indonesia. There are three species, one of which found in India. The Killer Catfishes thrive in large rivers, tanks and lakes, and especially in jheels with grassy margins, and are one of the largest, and most voracious and predatory of the local catfishes. The fish prefers muddy tanks that are subject to periodic flooding from a river. It is a pre-monsoon summer breeder. It grows to about 2m in length and weighs more than 45kg. It is rather sluggish and stays at the bottom of the water in search of food. If handled, it bites strongly as it has a huge mouth with formidable jaws, armed with bands of conical teeth. In India it is offered as a sacrifice to the Goddess Kali by the Hindus.

Family Schilbeidae: Schilbid Catfishes

Approximately 16 genera are equally divided between Africa and Asia. Most of the Asian genera are restricted to the Indian subcontinent, and there are seven in the Indian subregion. In India, these catfishes constitute a striking and well-marked group. Some of them are amongst the largest freshwater fishes of Asia. Little study has been devoted to these economically valuable fishes which are known to undertake spawning migrations up some rivers such as the Mahanadi, Narmada and Tapti.

Subfamily: Schilbeinae

Genus Pseudeutropius: Glass Catfishes The Striped Glass Catfish is one of the two species found in India. Its bright colour and small size have attracted the attention of aquarists.

Family Pangasiidae: Tiger Shark Catfish

Genus Pangasius: This family ranges from the Indian subcontinent (including the Indus basin but not Sri Lanka), through mainland southeast Asia, Sumatra and Borneo. Of the six genera, there is only one genus with one species in India. In appearance the Indian Tiger Shark resembles the Shilbelid, *Silonia silondia*, but can be readily distinguished from it by the absence of caniniform teeth on the jaws and by the presence of two pairs of fairly well-developed barbels. This catfish grows upto 1.5m and inhabits the lower portions of large rivers, particularly estuaries where it breeds during the rains. It feeds on foul and decaying animal and vegetable matter.

Family Amblycipitidae: Scissorstail Catfishes

These small fishes inhabit the swift streams of southern Asia (Pakistan to southern Japan). Two genera are in the Indian region.

Genus Amblyceps: The Scissorstail Catfish has an elongated body with a small, broad head which is depressed and covered with thick skin. The mouth is wide with four pairs of barbels. This catfish inhabits pebbly beds in swift-flowing streams at the foot of hills.

Family Akysidae: Stream Catfishes

Akysids are minute, subtly-coloured, secretive Catfishes with tiny eyes, encountered singly or in small numbers in the freshwaters of southern Asia. There are three genera, one found in the Indo-Burmese region.

Genus Akysis: The fishes of this genus are diminutive inhabitants of mountain streams and lakes. There are six recognised species of which two are found in the Indian region.

Family Sisoridae: Sisorid Catfishes

Sisoridae is an exclusively Asian family of bottom-dwelling Catfishes, most with more-or-less thickened leathery skins. They range in size from 20mm to 2m. These fish have granulated skins, or sometimes the skins are smooth but give the appearance of being mottled. These catfishes have adhesive labial or thoracic organs with which they cling to the substrate. The family has its greatest diversity in the Indian subcontinent. Of approximately 20 genera, 18 are in the Indian region.

Genus Bagarius: Giant Catfishes *Bagarius* differs from all other Sisoridae and, perhaps, from all other catfishes in the following two characteristics:
- The maxillary bone of each side is composed of two ossifications instead of a single ossification
- The teeth in the lower jaw are *heterodont*, that is, of different kinds (incisors, molars etc) as in mammals. This genus is endemic to the Oriental region. There are three species, two in the Indian region. Externally the two Indian species are very similar and this, together with the variability in colouration in *B. yarrellii*, explains why they have only recently been recognised as separate species. The Painted Giant Catfish is the giant of the two; it is one of the largest Asian catfishes and, so far, is the largest member of the Sisoridae. It grows to more than 2m and attains a weight of 135kg. This fish lies mostly at the bottom of the water and can even withstand the forceful current amongst rocks. The breeding season is prior to the start of the monsoon rains. The name 'Fresh Water Shark' is often applied to this fish because of its voracious feeding habits and overslung mouth. It is the most powerful fish of the freshwaters of India.

Genus Conta: Thread Tail Catfishes Of these fish, only two species are endemic to India. The Thread Tail Catfish in its general characteristics, habits and habitat seems much like the other Loach-like catfishes of the genus *Olyra* and *Amblyceps* and has been collected as the latter from the same stream. This rather rare catfish attains a length of 7.8cm.

Genus Glyptothorax: Torrent Catfishes This genus is primarily Oriental but extends into West Asia as far as Turkey. Sisorid catfishes of this genus inhabit foothill rivers and mountainous swift-flowing streams. They are benthic fishes, attaching themselves to the bottoms of rivers by means of a thoracic sucking disc. Of about 60 species, 30 are in the Indian region. Famous amongst them is the Copper Catfish.

Genus Hara: Belly Sucker Catfishes The genus *Hara* is closely allied to the genus *Erethistes* from which it is primarily distinguished by the nature of the pectoral spine. This genus is endemic to South Asia. All four species are in the Indian region. The Giant Moth Catfish is the largest of the four and is quite rare.

Genus Laguvia: Flat Headed Catfishes This genus comprises small fishes which usually inhabit rapid-running waters at the foot of mountains. The four species are all found in the Indian region. The Cheetah Catfish is a vividly-marked dwarf catfish which attains a length of 3cm. The fish of this group are quite delicate and require the care of the experienced aquarist to do well in captivity.

Genus Nangra: Broad Headed Catfishes This genus is endemic to South Asia. It was merged with the genus *Hara* but, in 1963, Tilak came to the conclusion that the two genera are osteologically distinct. Three species are all found in the Indian region. The Brilliant Catfish is indeed brilliant.

Genus Sisor : Whiptail Catfishes This monotypic genus is endemic to South Asia. This family has four pairs of barbels but this species has often been reported to possess six pairs of barbels. The outer mandibular pair consists of several barbels which are often joined together at their base by a flap. This unusual catfish attains a length of 18cm.

Family Clariidae : Airbreathing Catfishes

This distinctive family of air-breathing fishes of Africa and Asia is readily distinguished by its elongated, entirely spineless dorsal fin, arborescent air-breathing apparatus, elongated anal fin and distinctive overall appearance. Air-breathing apparatus arises from gill-arches 2 and 4 and is undoubtedly responsible for the ability of this fish to live in very oxygen-poor waters and also out of water for much longer than other catfishes. There are some 15 genera; two in the Indian region.

Genus Clarias: The Walking Catfish is abundant in ponds and rivers, and lies concealed for hours in the mud. It is found in all types of waters but more so in derelict and swampy areas. It can live out of water for quite some time and moves short distances over land as it has an accessory respiratory organ. This is a rather hardy fish. It attains a length of 46cm and in captivity lives for a number of years, often being utilised as a test animal for the biological assay of pituitary hormones. The air-bladder yields a coarse isinglass. The species has a short spawning period during July and August, coinciding with the Southwest monsoons. It also breeds in the confined

This swamp in Dinhata (Northern Bengal) contained Channa Marulius, amongst other species of Puntius and Chandra.

waters of ponds and tanks and often migrates to nearby flooded pools and puddles for breeding during the rainy season. Inundated paddy fields are the most preferred spawning grounds.

Family Heteropneustidae: Stinging Catfishes

These fishes live in stagnant pools and ditches deficient in oxygen. The pectoral spines have an associated venom gland and this fish is considered dangerous to persons wading in its territory. The family is represented by a single genus confined to freshwaters ranging from Pakistan to Thailand (primarily India, Sri Lanka, Bangladesh and Myanmar).

Genus Heteropneustes: This genus is widely distributed in the Oriental region and the two species are both found in the Indian region. The Asian Stinging Catfish is a fish of great economic importance. Its air-breathing apparatus enables it to exist in almost any kind of water so it is found in ponds, ditches, swamps and marshes, and sometimes found in muddy rivers. It is able to tolerate slightly brackish water. It lives in large shoals in suitable localities and is extensively fished because its flesh reputedly has invigorating qualities. During the dry season 'Singi', as it is called locally, lives in semi-liquid and semi-dry mud, and even when the mud dries up it sinks to the bottom of the fissures and crevices formed by the cracking mud. These fishes breed in confined waters during the monsoon months. Spawning has been observed in swampy patches falling within the flood regions of rivers. This fish, which attains a length of 30cm, is in great demand because of its 'medicinal' value. Fishermen stock tanks with 'Singi' during the rainy season. In the Calcutta markets live fishes are sold in large quantities. Boat-loads of living fish are brought from the deltaic districts and the Sunderbans. In the summer months (April–June) about 90% of 'live fishes' consist of Singi and Clarius. This fish is dreaded because of its aggressive behaviour and can inflict painful wounds with its potentially dangerous pectoral spines.

Family Chacidae: Squarehead or Angler Catfishes

These fishes are robust but ugly to look at. This small family consists of a single genus restricted to the Indian sub-continent and the Malay Peninsula.

Genus Chaca: The Devil Catfish is quite popular with aquarists despite its grotesque appearance. The body is flat and stumpy, the head broad and depressed. The mouth is very wide. The dorsal fin is small, with two spines and four soft rays. There are three species; two are found in the Indian region.

Family Olyridae: Fighting Catfishes

The Fighting Catfishes have elongated bodies which are naked; their eyes are small and the nostrils are wide apart. This family comprises specialised hillstream fishes of a single genus only, confined to India, Myanmar and Western Thailand.

Genus Olyra: The Long Fighting Catfish won the third prize at Aquarama '93. It could be called the 'Siamese Fighting Bettas' of the catfishes – no two specimens could be kept in a single aquarium as they would fight to the death.

Family Ariidae: Sea Catfishes

These medium-to-large catfishes inhabit coastal waters, particularly river mouths, but many of the species enter freshwater and some only occur in freshwater. These are dangerous fishes as the serrated spines inflict painful lacerated wounds. There are no poison glands, but the mucous on the spine is toxic. Six of the 20 genera are found in the Indian region, of which five occur in inland waters.

Genus Arius: Shark Catfishes The fishes of this genus are primarily marine, but some species are confined to freshwaters. The Indian species of this group was previously known under the generic name of Tachysurus Lacepede. The number of species is large and most of them are very abundant and economically important. The Dusky Shark Catfish is quite popular in aquaria.

Family Plotosidae: Eel Tail Catfishes

These catfishes occur in marine, brackish water and freshwaters of tropical and warm–temperate regions. There are five species, three in the Indian region.

Genus Plotosus The Eel Catfish can attain a length of 150cm and is commonly found at 80cm. These are quite shy fish and require to be kept in dimly-lit aquaria.

ORDER: BATRACHOIDIFORMES

Family Batrachoididae: Toad Fishes

The Toad Fishes are primarily coastal benthic in temperate to tropical seas, a few species entering brackish water. There are three subfamilies of which only one (Batrachoidinae) is represented in the Indian area, and of the 15 genera in this sub-family, only two occur in the Indian region.
Genus Batrichthys There are four species, one in the Indian region. The Gangetic Toad Fish attains a length of 30cm. Its spine may inflict wounds to people handling it. It makes deep grunting sounds when disturbed, the reason for this is not known.

ORDER: CYPRINODONTIFORMES

Most species of this group are surface feeding fishes and about 75% live in fresh or brackish water. The members of this order are secondary freshwater fishes and are found throughout tropical and temperate latitudes. They are especially notable for the range of freshwater and saline habitats they occupy.

Suborder Exocoetoidei

Of the four families, three are in the Indian region and only two inhabit Indian freshwaters. The fishes of the third family, Exocoetidae (Flying Fishes), are usually found offshore.

Family Hemiramphidae: Halfbeaks

The Halfbeaks live near the surface and are protectively coloured for environment by being green or blue on the back and silvery-white on the sides and ventrally. The tip of the lower jaw usually is bright red or orange. Most species are marine but some inhabit brackish and freshwater sites. Some species are live-bearers; in these species a part of the anal fin is modified as an organ which can be inserted into the female in order to fertilise the eggs. The freshwater forms are all viviparous, in contrast to the salt-water species. The circumtropical Hemiramphidae and Halfbeaks comprise about 12 genera, three in inland waters of the Indian region.

Genus Dermogenys: This genus is chiefly distinguished by a dorsal fin situated a short distance behind the anal fin. *Dermogenys*, found in brackish as well as freshwater habitats, are the most widely distributed of the viviparous Southeast Asian Halfbeaks, ranging from India, Myanmar and Thailand along the coast of the Malay Peninsula and greater Sunda Islands to Celebes. Several species are recognised, two in the Indian region.

Genus Xenentodon The genus is widely distributed in freshwater areas in Pakistan, India, Bangladesh, Sri Lanka, Myanmar, Thailand, the Malay Peninsula, Sumatra and Western Borneo. There are probably three species, two in the Indian region of which one is still undescribed. The Long Nose Needle Fish is an elegant surface-living fish which reaches a length of 40cm. In North Bengal it occurs in clear, gravelly, perennial streams and ponds of the Terai and Duars. It is fairly common in the Ganga-Brahmaputra system.

Suborder Asrianichthyodei

Of the three families, two are found in the Indian region.

Family Oryziidae: Medakas or Ricefishes

A single genus is found in fresh and brackish waters of India and the Indo-Australian archipelago. They are small (maximum length about 9cm), usually surface-living fishes, inhabiting a great variety of different waters.

Genus Oryzias: The relationship of *Oryzias* with other Cyprinodontiformes is based on osteological characteristics. These inhabit fresh and brackish waters and are useful in that they eat mosquito larvae. There are seven species, but only one in India, the Blue Eyes. This delicate, translucent, little killifish is widely distributed in India and Myanmar. In the Andaman Islands it was accidently introduced with fry. The fish matures earlier in brackish than in freshwaters, and grows up to 4cm in length. It is a perennial breeder particularly from November to March. The eggs remain attached to the flattened genital pad of the female and are carried about by the mother until they hatch.

Suborder Cyprinodontoidei
Family Aplocheilidae: Rivulines

These typically small fishes average an adult size of 8–10cm standard length and inhabit fresh and brackish water of Africa, Southern Asia and southern North America. They are markedly sexually dimorphic. Of approximately 15 genera, only one is found in the Indian area. Two more were imported and introduced into freshwaters as they are hardy and successful larvivorous fishes.

Genus Aplocheilus: Panchax Males are larger than females, often with fin extensions. In many cases the pigment pattern is composed of several dark crossbars on the sides of the body as is evident in the beautiful Striped Panchax. All the species have a spot at the anterior base of dorsal fin. Most species do well in captivity but would swallow whole smaller fishes. There are five species, four in the Indian region.

Family Poecilidae: Guppies and Mollies

These are naturally restricted to the New World fishes, ranging from Illinois and New Jersey in the United States to Argentina. Two members of this family were at different times introduced into India for antimalarial work.

Genus Gambusia: Mollies This species was introduced into India in 1928 from Italy for antimalarial work and has readily taken to Indian waters. The species is predacious and active for its size (6.2cm). It is a livebearer with a great appetite for its own young, and it is hardy, able to withstand all types of foul water conditions and poor food. It has a temperature tolerance from above freezing point to 300°C. It is reported to be able to consume mosquito larvae equal to its own weight in a day. Dr Menon (1966, 1977) is of the opinion that it is dangerous to introduce this species during an antimalarial campaign in places where it does not occur naturally since it is very destructive in a new habitat. Today, *Gambusia affinis* has the widest distribution of any freshwater fish in the world, largely as a result of mosquito control programmes.

Genus Poecilia: Guppies The best known and by far the most popular of the ovoviviparous or livebearing fishes, the guppy has probably introduced more aquarists to their hobby than all the other tropical fishes combined. It is physically attractive, active, prodigiously fertile, extremely hardy, altogether peaceable, and capable of thriving in almost any temperature, confined spaces and near stagnant waters. It is the "beginner's" species. In its almost infinite variety, it retains interest even for the most sophisticated aquarists. Hybridized in countless combinations and permutations, most of the guppies commercially available today bear little or no resemblance to the nondescript wild guppy from which they derive. It was introduced into India from South America in 1908, for mosquito control. Besides its beauty, the guppy has other great merits. It is a livebearer and is an extremely fertile as well as dependable breeder. It is unusually active. The most striking feature of sexual behaviour in this species is the manner in which the males persistently pursue the females with a quick thrust of the highly modified anal fin or gonopodium.

ORDER SYNGNATHIFORMES

The members of this group are noted not only for their bizarre appearance but also for their strange anatomical and biological characteristics, which clearly sets them apart from all other fishes. One feature that they all have in common is a long, tube-shaped snout. There are seven families, all in the Indian region but only one is found in inland waters. The family Pegasidae, represented by *Pegasus volitans*, has been listed from estuarine waters in the Indo-West Pacific but not in the Indian region. The fishes of the family Pegasidae are characteristic with a depressed head and body, abdominal pelvic fins and enlarged wing-like pectoral fins.

Family Syngnathidae: Sea Horses and Pipefishes

These fishes are wide-ranging in their distribution. Most are found in estuarine and coastal marine areas, but breeding populations occur throughout the salinity range from fresh to hypersaline waters. Although commonly portrayed in the decorative motifs of fabrics and artwork these fishes have little economic value in India. They have been used in the preparation of medicines and aphrodisiacs in some parts of the Orient, and sometimes they are dried or embedded in plastic and sold as curios. There are 47 genera presently recognised of which 15 inhabit the Indian region, although only four can be found in the inland waters.

Genus Microphis: Pipefishes With the exception of two Atlantic subspecies of M. Brachyurus, all the rest are distributed within the Indo-Pacific. Juveniles and subadults may occur in oceanic and estuarine localities, but juveniles and adults of all taxa are apparently most common in freshwater streams and rivers. Eighteen species are recognised, six in the Indian region.

Among the gastrophorine (trunk pouch) syngnathids there are two groups of so-called 'freshwater' pipefishes which are generally similar in gross morphology and typically have nine caudal fin-rays. One of these, reviewed by Dawson (1981), includes four species of the Indo-Pacific genus *Doryichthys* which has not been reported from the Indian region. The second group, represented by the genus Microphis, is characterised in having the lateral trunk ridge confluent with interior tail ridge.

ORDER SYNBRANCHIFORMES

These are eel-like fishes of small to moderate size, attaining a maximum length of about 1m. They are burrowing and prefer a cavernicolous habitat. They lack pelvic and pectoral fins and the caudal fin is reduced or absent. The members of this order are usually adapted for life in ponds, ditches and swamps.

Family Synbranchidae: Swamp Eels

Synbranchids occur in a variety of habitats, both fresh and brackish water. Many species live in swamps or marshy areas, where burrowing and amphibious habits are commonly displayed, although the same species may be found in streams, rivers, ponds or lakes. These are pantropical, usually restricted to freshwater. Although called 'eel' because of their appearance, the synbranchids are thought to be closely related to Mastacembelidae. There are four genera, two in the Indian region.

Genus Monopterus: There are seven species, five of which are found in India. The Giant Swamp Eel attains a length of 60cm and is fairly common in the Duars (N. Bengal) where it is relished as a food fish. The Rice Swamp Eel, which attains a length of 45cm, is able to survive in deep mud pockets during the dry season when the water in the ponds evaporates It spawns during the summer months and builds a bubble nest in which the eggs float at the surface.

Genus Ophisternon: Mud Eels There are six species, one in the Indian region. The Black Cylindrical Eel is very common in West Bengal, growing to about 100cm in length. This fish is an efficient burrower. It is also found in brackish water areas.

ORDER SCORPAENIFORMES
Suborder Platycephalidae: Flatheads
These are benthic fishes comprising of about 12 genera, eight of which are found in the Indian region. Of these two are found in estuarine waters.

Genus Platycephalus There are 13 species, two of which are found in India. The Striped Tailed Alligator Fish is quite popular with aquarists. This fish won the 3rd prize at Aquarama '93. They swallow whole small fish and thrive well in fine sandy-bottomed tanks.

ORDER PERCIFORMES
Most Perciformes have the following characteristics in common: dorsal, anal and pelvic fins, spines.

The Perciformes is the largest order of fishes, comprising about 150 families and some 7800 species. About one-third of all fish species are Perciformes. This order is an unnatural (polyphyletic) assemblage of spiny-headed fish (acanthopterygians) that have attained a vaguely defined 'grade' of evolution and lack the specialisations of the various derivative orders. Without any unique specialised characteristics to serve as diagnostic features of this order, membership of the Perciformes is uncertain at best. About 75% of all Perciformes are marine shore fishes while about 14% normally occur only in freshwater. Forty families of Perciformes are represented in the Indian inland waters but most of these include fishes that visit sporadically, spawning only in the sea and not ascending rivers as part of an obligatory migration.

Suborder Percoidei
This suborder, the largest of the Perciformes, contains 73 families, 589 genera and about 3524

species. Approximately 26% of the species normally occur only in freshwater. The majority of these are Cichilds and Percids.

Family Centropomidae: Barramundis

These are medium-to-large bottom-living fishes found in coastal waters, estuaries and lagoons. Most species are partial to brackish water. There are four genera, two in the Indian region.

Genus Lates: Sea Perches There are eight species; seven are African and confined to freshwaters, and one is marine or estuarine and widely distributed in the Indo-Pacific from India and Bangladesh, Myanmar to Australia, Southern China and Japan. The Giant Sea Perch is a coastal and estuarine species. It enters estuaries and backwaters in pursuit of food and shelter but always returns to the marine environment for spawning. Juveniles of this species frequent the lower estuarine areas of the Hoogly-Matla river system and enter impoundments with the tidal water which acts as the main source of fry for brackish water culture in impoundments popularly known as 'Bhasabadha' fisheries in West Bengal. This prime estuarine perch comes into the Chilka Lake (Orissa) as a young fish and goes back to the sea for breeding in June/July. The maximum size attained is 150cm, though a more usual size is 45–60cm. The air-bladders are made into rough isinglass.

Family Ambassidae: Glassfishes

These are small translucent, brilliant silvery fishes found throughout the Indo-West Pacific region and are common in estuaries and freshwaters. These fishes are not very good to eat but make excellent bait; they are easily dried without the need to use salt owing to their formation, and are used as manure for the cultivation of crops. They are also greatly valued in the control of guineaworm disease through their cyclopsidal activities and are also efficient agents for biological control of mosquitoes. The body is 'glassy' or semi-transparent with the vertebral column and swimbladder easily visible in the living fish, hence giving rise to the name 'Glassfishes'.

Ambassidae is one of the few families of percoid fishes which exhibit greater diversity in freshwater than in marine habitats. Eight of the nine genera currently recognised and about 21 of the approximately 41 species are confined to freshwaters in Madagascar, South Asia, southeast Asia and the Australian region.

Genus Chanda: Long Glassfishes The Elongated Glass Perchlet contributes to the artisanal fish catches in Uttar Pradesh, Bihar and West Bengal. It attains a length of 11cm. These small, long, bony fishes are sold in heaps, together with other small fishes, as cheap food in the fish markets.
Genus Parambassis: Giant Glassfishes These are found in the freshwater streams of southeast Asia and the Indo-Australian Archipelago. There are eight species, two in India.
Genus Pseudambassis: Jewel Glassfishes These small, transparent fishes inhabit the freshwaters of Pakistan, India, Bangladesh, Myanmar and Thailand. They are prized as attractive aquarium fishes and also are eaten locally. The Jewel Glassfish is a fascinating fish that resembles a bit of amber-coloured crystal moving about the aquarium. It attains a maximum length of 7cm. This delightful aquarium novelty makes a nest and guards its young. It breeds everywhere during the rains.

Family Teraponidae: Tiger Perches

Terapons inhabit Indo-Pacific inshore marine and brackish waters, some species also entering freshwaters. Most of the freshwater species occur in Australia where they are the third largest freshwater group. There are 15 genera, two in the Indian area.

Genus Terapon:Target Fishes The three species are all marine, but enter into brackish and freshwaters. The Target Fish is a very robust and hardy fish for the aquaria. It attains a length of 25cm. However, a word of caution – these fishes target all other fish in the aquaria, irrespective of size.

Family Sillaginidae: Sillagos

This small family of fishes lives in the sandy shores and estuarine waters of the Indo-Pacific. It is closely related to the family Sciaenidae in most essential characters; but may be recognised by the vomerine teeth and in having the lower part of the preopercle sharply angled inwards to meet that of the other side, thus forming the ventral surface of the head. There are three genera, two in the Indian region.

Genus Sillaginopsis: Aerial Fishes This is monotypic genus. The Aerial Fish attains a length of 44cm, and is a commercially-important fish captured by nets and longlines in the Hoogly estuary. It probably spawns in the Hoogly twice a year during the months November–February and August–September and the juveniles migrate towards the upper reaches during March, April and December, where they remain for two or three months.

Genus Sillago: Antenna Fish There are 24 species, nine in India, of which two species positively inhabit inland waters. The Antenna Fish is a near-shore species that frequently penetrates estuaries for considerable distances. This species is a permanent inhabitant of the Chilka Lake (Orissa) and goes out to the sea or the mouth of the lake for breeding which takes place by about February. Juveniles are in the lake from the close of winter until the rainy season. The maximum size attained is 25–30cm.

Family Lutjanidae: Snappers

Generally marine, Snappers are very occasionally found in estuaries. There are 17 genera, 13 in the Indian area of which only one is found in the estuaries.

Genus Lutjanus There are about 65 species of which 26 are found in India and only two in estuarine waters.

Family Lobotidae: Tripletails

The Lobotids inhabit inshore saltwater, as well as brackish and freshwaters. They are found throughout the tropical Indo-Pacific and in the tropical Atlantic. The young camouflage themselves by acting like leaves, turning sideways and floating at the surface. The two genera are both found in the Indian region.

Genus Datnioides: The fishes of this genus are found in fresh and brackish waters in southeast Asia and the tropical Australian region (especially New Guinea). There are three species of which only one is found in the Indian region. The Six-Banded Tiger was until recently fairly common in the estuaries of the Ganga and rivers of Myanmar but, since 1996, populations at various collecting areas have dwindled considerably and no sighting of this fish was reported during the whole of 1997. The cause of this depletion is the heavy industrial pollution of the rivers where this fish is found. It is a voracious predator growing to 30cm. It is not four-barred as the name implies (*D. quadrifasciatus*), but bears six to eight bands, which coalesce as the fish ages.

Family Monodactylidae: Finger Fishes

These are medium sized fishes occurring in large shoals in estuaries and over shallow reefs. They are equally at home in fresh and salt water. The Malayan Angel is beautiful but not as gaudy as some other aquarium fishes. This handsome creature is one of the very few marine fish that can be kept in freshwater aquaria with no apparent ill-effects.

Family Scatophagidae: Scats

Scats are small estuarial fishes found in harbours, estuaries and the lower reaches of freshwater rivers. It is generally believed that these fishes, like the archer fishes, spawn in the neighbourhood of coral reefs but that the young migrate to the freshwaters at the mouths of rivers and estuaries until they grow large enough to go back to the sea. Scatophagus pass through a larval phase called the Tholichthys stage, in which a strong bony armouring of the head and nape is developed, which regresses later. Scats collect in great numbers about the sewerage outfalls of large towns and anywhere else where the water brings down human refuse. The fish are disc-shaped, deep and compressed. The head and mouth are small. These are commonly referred to by aquarium retailers as the 'poor man's Discus'. There are two genera, one found in the Indian region.

Genus Scatophagus: Some fishes have red spots arranged in various patterns on the back. Such forms are known as *S.rubrifrons*. These fishes attain a length of 30cm and are quite common in Indian backwaters.

Family Nandidae: Leaffishes

The Nandids exhibit extreme morphological specialisations correlated with exceptionally well-developed predatory habits. At rest, most look deceptively like drifting leaves. It is generally accepted that this family exhibits the most disrupted geographical distribution known in freshwater teleosts of the primary division. The Nandids differ technically from other related families chiefly in features of the skeleton. All, except Badis, have the peculiar feature of having the caudal and rear ends of the dorsal and anal fins so transparent as to be hardly visible in the live fish.

The family comprises a fascinating group of relatively small fishes, most of which are well known to the tropical fish hobbyist. Members of this family are found in three continents, Africa, South America and Southeast Asia, in fresh, occasionally brackish, water. There are seven genera in three subfamilies in the Indian region.

Subfamily Nandinae

There are five genera of which only one is found in the Indian area.

Genus Nandus: Leaffish This species is common in ditches and flooded fields and attains a length of 20cm. These fish will gulp down fish slightly smaller than themselves, so care should be taken by the aquarist.

Subfamily Pristolepidinae: Sunfishes

These fishes inhabit a small area of peninsular India and Sri Lanka, Southeast Asia and parts of the Malay archipelago.

Genus Pristolepis: Two species are found in the southern part of India. These rare fish are quite attractive to look at and could become popular with aquarists.

Subfamily Badinae: Dwarf Chameleon Fishes
The fishes of this family are confined to Pakistan, Nepal, Bangladesh and Myanmar and are monotypic.

Genus Badis: This is one of the most interesting and colourful fish in this family because of its amazing range of pigmentation. Its colour changes are often made with great rapidity, and vary from solid colours to intricate mottled designs. Superficially it resembles the cichlids to which it is not related, although its breeding habits are similar to many members of that family. This is the most beautifully-coloured of all Badinae. This solitary predatory fish spends much of its time motionless, lurking in wait for moving animals. It shows no special colour when feeding other than appearing to have a marbled or mottled appearance. The adult males are highly territorial. One subspecies, the Red Chameleon Fish, attains a maximum length of 8cm. These are column feeders and feed on mosquito larvae when given the opportunity. In the aquarium it has a habit of remaining at the bottom and nibbling at vegetable detritus. It is shy with highly-changeable colouration and markings.

Family Cichlidae: Cichlids

Cichlids form an important group of relatively large and often colourful aquarium fishes. They are hardy and aggressive, distributed through South America, northward to Texas, and are also found in Africa. A single genus *(Etroplus)* is found in India and Sri Lanka. One of their principal identifying marks is a single nostril on each side rather than double nostrils. It is the second largest family in the Perciformes. There are about 85 genera, one in the Indian region and another two introduced into Indian freshwaters.

Genus Etroplus: Chromides These inhabit both brackish and freshwaters of peninsular India as far north as Orissa and south to Sri Lanka. The Banded Chromide was introduced into the aquarium trade during Aquarama '97. This is a very rare fish and is found in a single river in the state of Karnataka. Commercial collection of this species is virtually impossible, leaving breeding as the eventual solution towards making this beautiful fish available to aquarists. The Green Chromide or Pearl Spot is a brackish water species which attains a length of 40cm. These are very common in the backwaters of Kerala, Tamil Nadu, Andhra Prdesh and Orissa and are highly prized as food fish. It is extensively cultivated in ponds and tanks where it breeds naturally and it thrives well where luxuriant growth of aquatic vegetation is available. These fishes attain 10–12cm and 113gm in the first year in the ponds. Sexual maturity is attained in the second year. The females guard the fertilised eggs.

Genus Oreochromis: Mouthbreeders These are fish from East Africa which were introduced in August 1952 and are presently cultured in freshwater ponds in the country. The Tilapias are warm-water food fishes cultivated in over 30 developing countries. They are suitable for farming because they can be bred easily, and are hardy and high yielding. However, with the advent of floods these fish have entered nearly all the water bodies and are a major threat to small endemic species.

Suborder Mugiloidei

Family Mugilidae: Mullets The Mullets are remarkably uniform in external anatomy. Found throughout the world, inhabiting coastal waters, estuaries and rivers, these fishes are of commercial importance. Most species are typically coastal-estuarine and adaptable to great changes in salinity. Most species spawn at sea, and the young enter the nursery area (mainly estuaries), when they are about 10–15mm. There are 13 genera presently recorded from the inland waters.

Genus Liza: There are several species, seven in India. The Silver Mullet is a common mullet in the Hoogly-Matla estuary (West Bengal) and forms 0.4–0.9% of the total fish catch. In the Mahanadi (Orissa) estuary, it constitutes 6–9 % of the total catch, the fishing season being September–December. It grows up to 15–19cm in one year; a maximum length of 40cm is attained in natural waters and 25cm is common in ponds. Spawning takes place in the sea.

Genus Rhinomugil: This is monotypic. The Indian Anableps is a strange-looking fish with its protruding eyes. They are not very common, but many people in West Bengal and Orissa like to keep them in house ponds where they can be seen throughout the day floating near the surface of the water.

Suborder Polynemoidei
Family Polynemidae: Threadfins

The Threadfins (Tassel Fishes) are commercially-important suprabenthic fishes of sandy shores and muddy estuaries, well adapted to poor visibility with their projecting snouts, prolonged free pectoral rays and adipose eyelids. Of the seven genera, three are found in the Indian region.

Genus Eleutheronema: There are two species, one in India. The Fourfinger Threadfin inhabits sandy shores and muddy estuaries. It enters the estuary to breed when the salinity of the water starts rising. This species is an excellent food fish and ascends higher up the rivers than any of the other polynemids.

Suborder Gobioidei
These are carnivorous, often sluggish fishes of shallow waters from marine to freshwater conditions, especially estuaries and tide pools.

Family Gobiidae: Gobies
Gobiidae, probably the most numerous of all living fish families, is rather poorly represented in the freshwaters of the Indian region. These are small fishes, with most species being less than 10cm. There are few freshwater species, but numerous estuarine and coral reef species. This family contains the world's smallest fishes and vertebrates. There are 220 genera worldwide.

Subfamily Gobiinae
The body is oblong to elongate. The head is naked of scales between and before the eyes.

Genus Awaous: This tropical species is primarily found in freshwater and upper parts of estuaries. There are four species, two in the Indian region.

Genus Brachygobius: Bee Fishes Brachygobius differs from all other gobiids in having the simple first ray of the second dorsal fin segmented rather than unsegmented. There are eight species, most restricted to freshwater, but only one is found in the Indian region. The Bumblebee Goby attains a length of 2cm.

Genus Glossogobius: Sleepers Twenty species are found in tropical/subtropical freshwaters and estuaries. Two species are found in India. The Sleeper Goby attains a length of 30cm and is dangerous to keep with small fish which it would quickly swallow whole.

Genus Oligolepis: Sailfin Gobies These are found in muddy estuaries and coastal bays. There are two species in India. Although they are quite rare, they are peaceful and easy to keep and are very interesting with their almost lacy finnage.

Genus Stigmatogobius: Knight Gobies These are quite active fish. There are six species of this genus in the Indian area, five in the estuarine waters.

Subfamily Apocrypteinae
The body is very elongated and the head is compressed, mostly scaled above and laterally. Scales are cycloid.

Genus Apocryptes: This is a monotypic genus which attains a length of 15cm.

Genus Boleopthalmus: There are several species; five in the Indian region of which two occur in Indian waters. The Blue Spot Dragon is a grotesquely handsome fish. It attains a length of 15cm.

Genus Pseudapocryptes: The Banded Goby attains a length of 18cm. In the pre-monsoon months this species occurs in large numbers in the Hoogly estuary. There are two species, with only one in India. They do well in community aquaria, eating almost everything that is offered to them.

Genus Scartelaos: Hi-Fin Gobies There are probably three species, all found in the Indian region of which only one occurs in the inland waters. This is quite rare and a recent introduction to the aquarium trade. It is slaty-blue above, lighter below the head and back, with blackish spots. These attain a length of 12cm.

Subfamily Periophthalminae: Mudskippers
These Gobies are familiar creatures on mudflats in Indian coastal regions. The pectoral fins, with their elongated and well-developed muscular base, enable the fishes to move rapidly and to make surprising leaps out of the water.

Genus Periophthalmus: Several species are found in tropical muddy habitats, especially among mangroves, and they spend considerable time out of water. There are eight species in the Indian area, five in the inland waters.

Subfamily Sicydiaphiinae
Genus Gobiopterus: Neon Gobies Of the three species, one is in the Indian area. The Multispotted Neon Goby is fairly common in the Hoogly estuary (West Bengal), Chilka Lake (Orissa) and the Ennur backwaters (Tamil Nadu).

Genus Sicyopterus: Clown Gobies Three species are found in India. It is a very rare fish, but extremely easy to keep. These could be termed the most peaceful and hardy of all gobies.

Family Eleotrididae

These are small fishes, with most species growing to less than 20cm. They are usually benthic fishes found in the freshwater, estuarine and marine waters. These are found worldwide with some 40 genera, of which 14 are found in the Indian area.

Genus Butis: Flat Headed Gobies This tropical genus is found in the estuaries and lower reaches of rivers. There are about five species, four found in India. This fish has an unusual habit of using a fallen leaf as a cover under which it moves around and hunts for its prey at the surface of the water. This also helps to protect the goby from predators.

Genus Eleotris: Bicolor Gobies There are about 10–15 species of these pugnacious fish, three species occurring in inland waters. These have been around for some time in the aquarium trade but, due to their inactivity, they are not popular with aquarists.

Genus Odonteleotris: Armadillo Gobies There are three species but only one is found in the Indian region. This very interesting goby grows to about 10cm in length but is very rare.

Family Gobiodidae: Eel-like Gobies

These fishes inhabit marine, brackish and freshwaters. There are eight genera, four in the Indian region.
Genus Odontamblyopus: Fanged Dragons These are monotypic. These fishes attain a length of 25cm and have very long, sharp teeth, but they make intriguing pets.

Family Trypauchenidae: Burrowing Gobies
These fishes, like the closely-related Gobiids, live in shallow waters and often burrow in muddy bottoms of the Indo-Pacific region in marine, brackish and freshwaters. Some species are virtually blind. There are five genera, of which four are found in Indian waters.

Genus Trypauchen: Neon Dragons: This is a very rare fish and quite difficult to maintain in aquaria.

Suborder Anabantoidei
These fishes are freshwater and indigenous to Africa and southern Asia. Nearly all the species are useful in their native haunts as destroyers of mosquito larvae. Since only two or three are large enough to be considered as food fishes, it is seen that most anabantids are good aquarium fishes. Nearly all the labyrinths fishes are what are commonly known as 'bubblenest builders'. The distinctive suprabranchial organ is an auxillary breathing apparatus. Air taken in through the mouth passes through the labyrinth of blood vessels where capillaries absorb oxygen. As air is taken in at various intervals, old air is forced out of the labyrinth through the gill-covers. This organ has enabled many species to occupy submarginal or even anoxic waters. In most anabantids the male builds a nest of floating bubbles. Eggs are deposited in the bubbles and the male exhibits parental care.

Family Anabantidae: Climbing Perches

Genus Anabas: These fishes inhabit all kinds of freshwater, including large streams, but flourish most in canals, ditches, lakes, ponds and swamps. By means of its supplementary breathing apparatus, the climbing perch can thrive in water deficient in oxygen. Two species are now recognised, both found in India, and they are valuable food fish in West Bengal and Andhra Pradesh. These fishes are very hardy and can live out of water for protracted periods. Usually they are caught from low-lying swamps and marshy tracts as well as derelict pits, pools and puddles. The Climbing Perch is also caught during rainy weather when it can be found prowling about on wetland. In its natural habitat this fish can propel itself over dry land for great distances by 'walking' on its 'walking fins'. These fishes attain a length of 25cm or more in the wild.

Subfamily Macropodinae: Paradise Fishes

Genus Pseudosphromenus: Paradise Fishes These are found in the freshwaters of India, Sri Lanka, the Malay Peninsula and China, in lowland streams and estuaries. They live at the surface of the water, occasionally near the bottom, from where they rise to breathe air. Though they are vegetable feeders they will readily take all forms of live/dry foods.

Subfamily Trichogasterinae: Gouramies

There are four species found in India which are all very beautiful and peaceful fish. The most popular among them is the Dwarf Gourami. These lovely little fishes are often sold live in bottles of water outside schools in Calcutta and they thrive well in aquaria. The Dwarf Gourami attains 5cm in length and is the smallest and most beautiful of the genus.

Family Osphronemidae: Giant Gourami

Genus Osphronemus: One of the most celebrated of the Asian food fishes and an important species in freshwater aquaculture in tropical Asia, the Giant Gourami was first introduced into Calcutta from Java during the first half of the last century. A second importation was brought to Tamil Nadu from Mauritius in 1865, the breeding of which was reported in 1916. However, this fish only established itself well in India after new consignments were brought in 1916 from Java and Mauritius to Tamil Nadu. Subsequently, these fish were translocated from Tamil Nadu to several states such as Maharashtra, Punjab, West Bengal, Karnataka, Andhra Pradesh and Kerala.

This species is the only true gourami. It is a freshwater fish sensitive to cold and hence suitable for culture in tropical waters. Further, this fish is very hardy and copes well with transportation. It is a herbivorous fish but also eats insects, worms and shrimp. The Giant Gourami attains a large size (60cm) and a weight of more than 10kg. In open water, it breeds only during the dry season, but in confined waters throughout the year. Eggs are laid on nests of aquatic weeds and grasses at the shallow margins of the water and are hardly distinguishable from bird nests. The nests are guarded by the parents.

Suborder Channoidei
Family Channidae: Snakeheads

Fishes of this family can be recognised by the shape of the head which resembles that of a snake. The snakeheads inhabit mainly permanent shallow lentic waters (ponds and lakes); the larger species such as the Peacock Snakehead also inhabit rivers and large lakes. These fishes are air-breathers. They live for many hours, sometimes days, out of water and can migrate across land from one freshwater pool to another. These fishes can be kept alive for days in the minimum quantity of water, or even if only the respiratory apparatus and the body are kept moist. All are carnivorous. These fishes are monogamous and great parental care is exercised by the various species. Apparently most snakeheads produce pelagic eggs. The adults make a nest in a swampy area or backwater by clearing a space among dense, grassy vegetation. The eggs are spawned in the clear area, float to the surface, and are guarded by one or both parents. There are perhaps 25 species, three in tropical Africa and the rest found in Asia.

Genus Channa: These fishes are a very conspicuous element of fish life in almost every part of India, in lowland streams and canals, in upland and mountain streams and lakes, ponds and swamps. There are 23 species, eight in the Indian region. The Rainbow Snakehead was discovered as recently as 1991. It is one of the most beautiful of all aquarium fish and can be found in a remote area of northeast India. This fish was overlooked by Indian Zoological icthyologists and was eventually discovered by the world famous collector Heiko Bleher during one of his trips to India. Incidentally, along with the Georgette Snakehead these are the smallest of the group, hardly attaining a maximum length of 17 - 20cm.

ORDER MASTACEMBELIFORMES

Mastacembelids are perhaps the most highly modified percoid family which is entirely restricted to freshwater. Their relationship to other percoids are unknown. Mastacembelids occur in tropical Africa and Asia in a variety of freshwater habitats at high and low altitudes, and are common in riverine and lacustrine environments, streams and ponds.

Family Mastacembelidae: Spiny Eels

The name 'Spiny Eel' comes from the series of detached, depressible spines preceding the soft dorsal fin. Some of the Spiny Eels have the disagreeable habit, when picked up, of wriggling backwards, thus spiking the unsuspecting aquarist with the suddenly-erected spines. They are found in a variety of habitats; some species burrow in the substrate during the day or for certain months and have been found buried in soil in drying ponds. Many of the Spiny Eels are air-breathers and can survive in mud and oxygen-deficient water for an indefinite time. The largest of these, the Tyre Track Eel, reaches a length of 90cm, but most others are less than 45cm long when full grown.

Genus Macrognathus: Peacock Eels Until recently this genus was only represented by two species. As recently as August 1997, the author (Rao) discovered a new species, the Red Tailed Spiny Eel, in a restricted area in North Bengal. Members of this genus usually occur in lowland habitats and at moderate elevations in all the large river systems of the Indian subcontinent. They attain an average length of 36cm and are considered by the locals as wholesome fish to eat. These fish spend most of their time at the bottom, concealing themselves in the mud, and are considered good scavengers in the aquaria.

Genus Mastacembelus: Spiny Eels These are fishes of moderate to large size (over 50cm) and are widely distributed in southeast Asia, including the continental Islands of Indonesia. The Spiny

Brown Eel, a very rare fish of southern India, has recently been introduced to the aquarium trade. Mastacembelid eels are fairly active fish and make interesting pets to keep. However, the large ones are infamous for consuming smaller fish.

Family Chaudhuridae: Spineless Eels

Genus Chaudhuria: These are extremely small eels, growing to a maximum of 6cm in length. They are confined to the freshwaters of northeast India, Myanmar, Thailand, China, Taiwan and possibly Korea. There is only one genus, so far represented by a single species, Chaudhuria Caudata, the smallest mastacembeloid.

Family Pilaiidae: Subcylindrical Eels

This family is represented by two genera. Very little is known about these very inactive and uncommon fish.

Genus Pillaia: These little fish are very inactive and spend most of their time lying at the bottom, either buried in mud or clinging to some submerged vegetation along the edges of streams which have over-hanging vegetation. They are found only in those areas of the stream where the water is flowing very slowly. They avoid light and try to hide in the mud.

Genus Garo: This species has been found in the paddy fields of the Garo Hills and in the Kaziranga Wildlife Sanctuary of Assam, which is situated on the southern bank of the Brahmaputra river, very close to the Mikir Hills. This genus is represented by a single species; Garo Khajuriai.

ORDER PLEURONECTIFORMES

This is a very distinctive group and is chiefly marine. Young flatfish are bilaterally symmetrical and swim upright, but early in their development one eye migrates across the top of the skull to lie adjacent to the other eye. They then lie and swim on the eyeless (blind) side. Flatfishes are benthic and carnivorous.

Suborder Soleoidei
Family Cynoglossidae: Tongue Fishes

Tongue Fishes are found in the warm waters of all oceans (between 400 degrees latitude). Most species occur in shallow waters or estuaries; they are adept at burrowing in sand, for which their very compressed bodies are well suited.

Genus Cynoglossus: Forty-nine species are recognised, with 15 in the Indian region. Most of the species frequent salt and brackish waters but are never found in freshwater.

Family Soleidae: Soles

Soles are benthic, meritic fishes occurring in all oceans. There are about 30 genera, nine of which are found in the Indian region. Of these probably only two occur in estuarine waters.

Genus Euryglossa: These small Indian soles inhabit both salt and freshwater areas. Four species are found in the Indian area, but only two are reported from estuarine areas.

ORDER TETRAONDONTIFORMES
Family Tetraondontidae: Puffer Fishes

Tetraodontids are found throughout all tropical and temperate waters. Most species are marine, but several enter estuaries and some live only in freshwater. The Puffer is so-called because it can inflate its body by swallowing water or air to form an almost spherical, generally spiny, ball to deter predators. Of the 16 genera, six are found in the Indian region. The teeth are fused into a beak-like dental plate with a median suture giving two 'teeth' on each jaw, thus giving rise to the name Tetraodon, meaning 'four teeth'.

Genus Chelonodon: Brackish Puffers Three species are found in the Indian region. The Topaz Puffer is a brilliantly coloured fish which reaches a length of 17cm. This fish is hardy, attractive and not

The Sasha River at Assam.

too aggressive. It is a mid-water swimmer. On the contrary, the White Spotted Puffer is a vicious fish and seems to be hungry all the time.

Genus Tetraodon: Freshwater Puffers A single species, the Emerald Puffer, is found in India. These fishes prefer to stay at the bottom of the tanks with their tails curved inwards to their bodies. They have very smooth and soft skin and, when inflated, resembles table-tennis balls.

Genus Monotretus: Dwarf Puffers The Red Green Dwarf Puffer is a remarkable little fish. It has the least number of vertebrae – only six. These small fish rarely exceed 2cm in total length.

chapter 3

Atlas of Ornamental Indian Fishes

In order to include as many pictures as possible and bearing in mind the international nature of the publication, we have intentionally decided against including detailed textual descriptions. Instead, we have used international symbols and, in this way, the most important facts about the species and its care can be easily obtained.

Age
The last number in the code always stands for the age of the fish in the photograph.

❶ small (baby, juvenile colouration)

❷ medium (young fish/saleable size)

❸ large (half-grown/good saleable size)

❹ XL (fully grown/adult)

❺ XXL (breeder)

❻ show (show fish)

Size
cm.. approximate size these fish can reach as adults.

Temperature

Ⓒ 18–22°C (68–72°F) room temperature

Ⓒ 22–25°C (71–77°F) tropical fish

pH value

ⓟ pH 6, 5–7, 2

no special requirements (neutral)

ⓟ pH 5, 8–6, 5 prefers soft,

lightly acidic water

Ⓡ pH 7, 5–8, 5 prefers hard,

alkaline water

Lighting

◡ bright, plenty of light/sun

◓ not too bright

◕ almost dark

Food

omnivorous/dry food, no special requirements

food specialist, live food/frozen food

predator, feed with live fish

plant-eater, supplement with plant food

Swimming

😐 no special characteristics

🙂 in upper area/surface fish

🙁 in lower area/floor fish

Aquarium set up

only floor and stones, etc

stones/roots/crevices

plant aquarium + stones/roots

Behaviour/reproduction

keep a pair or a trio

school fish, do not keep less than 10

egg layer

live-bearers, viviparous

mouth-brooder

cave-brooder

bubblenest builder

algae-eater/glass cleaner
(roots + spinach)

non aggressive fish, easy to keep
(mixed aquarium)

difficult to keep, read specialist
literature beforehand

warning, extremely difficult,
for experienced specialists only

Minimum tank		Length (cm)	Capacity (cubic litres)
SS	super small	20–40	5–20
S	small	40–80	40–80
m	medium	60–100	80–200
l	large	100–200	200–400
L	XL	200–400	400–3000
xl	XXL	over 400	over 3000
			'show' aquarium

Scale

Black Knife Fish 25cm
Notopterus notopterus (Pallas) 1769
Range: throughout India

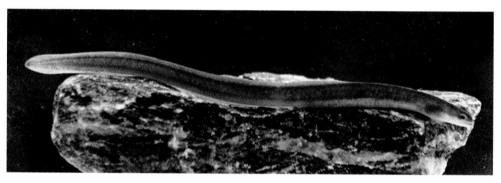

Brown Snake Eel 120cm
Anguilla bengalensis bengalensis (Gray) 1831
Range: east coast of India and Andaman Islands

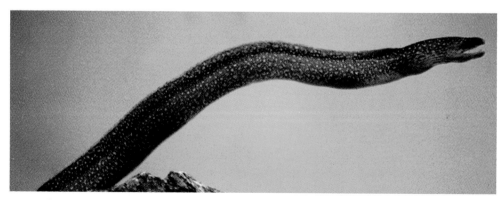

Spotted Moray Eel 60cm
Lycodontis tile (Hamilton-Buchanan) 1822
Range: Hoogly Estuary

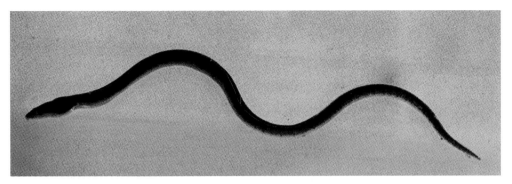

Olive Eel 70cm
Pisodonophis boro (Hamilton-Buchanan) 1822
Range: Indo-West Pacific

Thick Lips 120cm
Catla catla (Hamilton-Buchanan) 1922
Range: North and North-east India

Shovelmouth Carp 25cm
Chagunius chagunio (Hamilton-Buchanan) 1822
Range: Brahmaputra and Ganges drainages along the
Himalayan foothills

Red-Tail Grass Carp 99cm
Cirrhinus Mrigala mrigala (Hamilton-Buchanan) 1822
Range: Northern India

Red-Tailed Silver Shark 120cm
Gonoproktopterus curmuca (Hamilton-Buchanan) 1807
Range: Western Ghats

Sombre Barb 100cm
Gonoproktopterus thomassi (Day) 1873
Range: South Canara and Cardamom Hills

Scaly Barb 60cm
Gonoproktopterus lithopidos (Day) 1873
Range: South Karnataka

Black Line Shark 61cm
Labeo bata (Hamilton-Buchanan) 1822
Range: throughout India

Red Gilled Violet Shark 30cm
Labeo boga (Hamilton-Buchanan) 1822
Range: rivers of Gangetic Provinces

Syke's Shark 20cm
Labeo boggut (Sykes) 1838
Range: Northern India

All Black Shark 90cm
Labeo calbasu (Hamilton-Buchanan) 1822
Range: Northern India

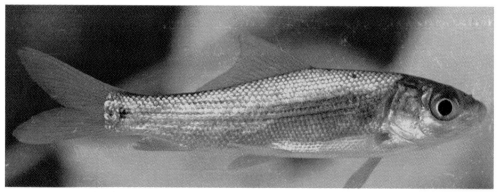

Miniscale Shark 120cm
Labeo gonius (Hamilton-Buchanan) 1822
Range: Assam

Silver Labeo 20cm
Labeo kawrus (Sykes) 1841
Range: Western Ghats

18Southern Orange Tailed Shark 61cm
Labeo kontius (Jerdon) 1849
Range: Cauvery River System

Pencil Gold Labeo 26cm
Labeo nandina (Hamilton-Buchanan) 1822
Range: Assam

Indian Rohu 180cm
Labeo rohita (Hamilton-Buchanan) 1822
Range: throughout India

Hi-Fin Barb 8cm
Oreichthys cosuatis (Hamilton - Buchanan) 1822
Range: Eastern India

Hi-Fin Variable 6cm
Oreichthys umangii (Rao) 1995
Range: Upper Assam

Diamond Barb 15cm
Osteobrama cotio cotio (Hamilton-Buchanan) 1822
Range: North-east India

Black Border Tail Orange Carp 18cm
Osteochilichthys nashii (Day) 1868
Range: Western Ghats of Karnataka

Hi-Fin Carp 20cm
Osteochilichthys longidorsalis (Pethyagoda Kotellat) 1993
Range: Western Ghats of Kerala

Four Spot Barb 12cm
Puntius arulius tambraparnei (Silas) 1953
Range: Tambraparnei River, Tamil Nadu

Two Spot Barb 6cm
Puntius bimaculatus (Bleeker) 1844
Range: Mysore

Green Swamp Barb 8cm
Puntius chola (Hamilton-Buchanan) 1822
Range: Northern India

Indian Rosy Barb 8cm
Puntius conchonius (Hamilton-Buchanan) 1822
Range: Eastern India

Red Line Torpedo Fish 15cm
Puntius (denisoni) umangii (Day) 1865
Range: Kerala

Long Snouted Barb 24cm
Puntius dorsalis (Jerdon) 1849
Range: Krishna River system

Melon Barb 6cm
Puntius fasciatus fasciatus (Jerdon) 1849
Range: Wynaad, Nilgiri Hill Range in Kerala and Karnataka

Black Spot Barb 12cm
Puntius fillamentosus madraspatensis (Jerdon) 1849
Range: Karnataka

DMK Fish 14cm
Puntius filamentosus lepidus (Day) 1869
Range: Kerala

Filament Barb 14cm
Puntius filamentosus assimilis (Jerdon) 1849
Range: South Kerala

Malini's Barb 18cm
Puntius mahecola (Day) 1878
Range: Anna Malai Hills

Golden Dwarf Barb 3cm
Puntius gelius (Hamilton-Buchanan) 1822
Range: Eastern and North East India

Streaked Barb 8cm
Puntius guganio (Hamilton-Buchanan) 1822
Range: North and Eastern India

Dwarf Barb 2.5cm
Puntius phutino (Hamilton-Buchanan) 1822
Range: Eastern India

Maharaja Barb 6cm
Puntius sahyadriensis (Silas) 1953
Range: Yenna River, Maharashtra

Sophore's Barb 8cm
Puntius sophore (Hamilton-Buchanan) 1822
Range: throughout Northern, Central and Eastern India

One Spot Barb 4cm
Puntius terio (Hamilton-Buchanan) 1822
Range: Northern India

Tic-Tac-Toe Barb 4cm
Puntius ticto (Hamilton-Buchanan) 1822
Range: throughout India

Kooli Barb 4cm
Puntius vittatus (Day) 1865
Range: Kerala

Double Mouth Tor 30cm
Schismatorhynchos nukta (Sykes) 1841
Range: Shimoga, Karnataka

Deccan Mahseep 46cm
Tor khudree (Sykes) 1839
Range: Central and South India

Neon Hatchet 5cm
Chela cachius (Hamilton-Buchanan) ? date
Range: Assam

Burjor's Brilliance 3cm
Chela dadiburjori (Menon) 1952)
Range: Kerala, Goa

Indian Glass Hatchet 5.5cm
Chela labuca (Hamilton-Buchanan) 1822
Range: throughout India

Silver Streak 8cm
Salmostoma phulo (Hamilton-Buchanan) 1822
Range: Gangetic and Brahmaputra drainages

Razorbelly 12cm
Salmostoma sardinella (Valenciennes) 1842
Range: Eastern India

Silver Carp 82cm
Hypohthalmichthys molitrix (Valenciennes) 1844
Range: introduced

Veli Lake Carplet 7cm
Amblypharyngodon chakaiensis (Babu and Nair) 1978
Range: Thiruvanthapuram District, Kerala

Brass Carplet 6cm
Amblypharyngodon mola (Hamilton-Buchanan) 1822
Range: most of India

Silver Minnow 15cm
Aspidoparia jaya (Hamilton-Buchanan) 1822
Range: Gangetic Provinces

Blue Dotted Hill Trout 15cm
Barilius bakeri (Day) 1865
Range: Western Ghats of Herala

Banded Hill Trout 7.5cm
Barilius barna (Hamilton-Buchanan) 1822
Range: Eastern India

Metallic Hill Trout 10cm
Barilius gatensis (Valenciennes) 1844
Range: Karnataka

Lineated Hill Trout 12.5cm
Barilius shacra (Hamilton-Buchanan) 1822
Range: Northern India

Spotted Hill Trout 15cm
Barilius tileo (Hamilton-Buchanan) 1822
Range: Eastern Himalayas

Half Banded Hill Trout 12.5cm
Barilius vagra (Hamilton-Buchanan) 1822
Range: Northern India

Zebra Danio 3cm
Brachydanio rerio (Hamilton-Buchanan) 1822
Range: West Bengal to Krishna River system

Giant Danio 10cm
Danio aequipinnatus (McClelland) 1839
Range: North-eastern India

Moustached Danio 8cm
Danio dangila (Hamilton-Buchanan) 1822
Range: Bihar and Assam

Turquoise Danio 5cm
Danio devario (Hamilton-Buchanan) 1822
Range: Eastern India

Malabar Danio 12cm
Danio malabaricus (Jerdon) 1849
Range: Western Ghats

South Indian Flying Barb 8cm
Esomus barbatus (Jerdon) 1849
Range: Tamil Nadu and Karnataka

Slender Rasbora 10cm
Parluciosoma daniconius (Hamilton-Buchanan) 1822
Range: throughout India

Black Line Rasbora 12cm
Parluciosoma labiosa (Mukerji) 1935
Range: Nasik District of Maharashtra

Yellowtail Scissorstail 12cm
Rasbora rasbora (Hamilton-Buchanan) 1822
Range: Assam and Karnataka

Glowlight Carplet 2cm
Hordandia atukorali (Deraniyagala) 1943
Range: Kerala

Slaty Algaeater 15cm
Crossocheilus latius latius (Hamilton-Buchanan) 1822
Range: most of India

Rhinocerous algaeater 10cm
Garra bicornuta (Rao) 1920
Range: Thunga River, Karnataka

Cardamom Algaeater 7.5cm
Garra hughii (Silas) 1955
Range: Cardamom and Palni Hills, Western Ghats

Kemp's Algaeater 11cm
Garra kempi (Hora) 1921
Range: Abor and Naga, Arunachal Pradesh

Khasi Algaeater 7.5cm
Garra lissorhynchus (McClelland) 1843
Range: Meghalaya

Cauvery Algaeater 17.5cm
Garra mcclellandi (Jerdon) 1849
Range: Cauvery River drainage

Brown Algaeater 17cm
Garra mullya (Sykes) 1841
Range: Peninsular India

Banded Torrent Fish 6cm
Psilorhynchus homaloptera (Hora and Mukerji) 1935
Range: Assam

Checkered Torrent Fish 5cm
Psilorhynchus sucatio (Hamilton-Buchanan) 1822
Range: North Bengal

Sparkling Torrent Fish 7cm
Psilorhynchus balitora (Hamilton-Buchanan) 1822
Range: Gomti River, Uttar Pradesh

Anamalai Sucker Loach 7cm
Homaloptera montana (Herre) 1945
Range: Anamalai Hills and Silent Valley

Angel Sucker Loach 10cm
Travancoria elongata (Pethyagoda-Kottellat) 1993
Range: Northern Travancore, Kerala

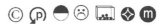

Sidewinder Loach 6cm
Aborichthys bijulensis (Rao) 1996
Range: Garo Hills, Meghalaya

Puma Loach 15cm
Acanthocobitis rubidipinnis (Blyth) 1861
Range: Tinsukia, Upper Assam

Leopard Loach
Acanthocobitis botia (Hamilton-Buchanan) 1822
Range: North-east India

Black Line Loach 6cm
Nemacheilus anguilla (Annandale) 1919
Range: Krishna River basin, South India

Banded Loach 4cm
Shistura beavani (Gunther) 1863
Range: North Bengal

Polka Dotted Loach 5cm
Schistura corica (Hamilton-Buchanan) 1822
Range: Cooch Behar, North Bengal

Ring Loach 5cm
Shistura denisoni dayi (Hora) 1935
Range: Chota Nagpur Plateau, Bihar

Olivaceous Loach 3cm
Schistura devdevi (Hora) 1935
Range: Teesta River drainage

Many Banded Loach 9.8cm
Schistura multifasciatus (Day) 1878
Range: Eastern Himalayas

Half Banded Loach 3cm
Schistura savona (Hamilton-Buchanan) 1822
Range: Kali River drainage in Uttar Pradesh

Victory Loach 8cm
Shistura scaturigina (McClennan) 1839
Range: Eastern sub-Himalayas

Fascinating Loach 5.5cm
Schistura semi armatus (Day) 1867
Range: Cauvery River basin in Wynaad, Southern India

Long Snouted Loach 8cm
Nemachilichthys ruppelli (Sykes) 1841
Range: Shimoga, Karnataka

Black Panther Loach 3cm
Shistura yenjitee (Rao) 1997
Range: Phuntsholing area of Bhutan

Grizzled Loach 2.7cm
Schistura sikmaiensis (Hora) 1921
Range: Manipur Valley

Zodiac Loach 6cm
Mesonoemacheilus triangularis (Day) 1865
Range: Western Ghats, Kerala

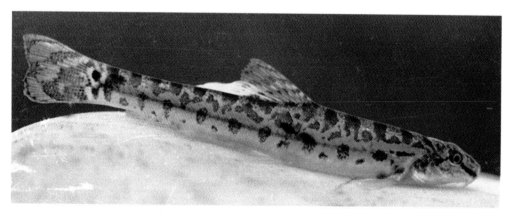

Tail Spot Loach 5cm
Lepidocephalus annandalei (Chaudhuri) 1912
Range: Upper Assam

Goalpara Loach 6cm
Lepidocephalus goalparensis (Pillai and Yazdani) 1976
Range: Goalpara District, Assam

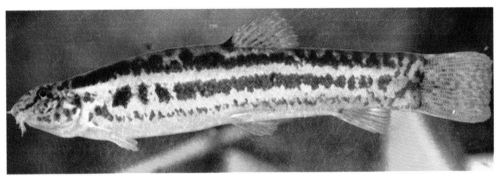

Panther Loach 6cm
Lepidocephalus gunthea (Hamilton-Buchanan) 1822
Range: most of Northern and Eastern India

Indian Coolie Loach 4.5cm
Pangio pangia (Hamilton-Buchanan) 1822
Range: North-east Bengal, Eastern Madhya Pradesh

Jaguar Loach 10cm
Somileptes gongota (Hamilton-Buchanan) 1822
Range: North Bengal and Assam

Y-Loach 6cm
Botia lohachata (Chaudhuri) 1912
Range: Indus and Ganga drainage

Tiger Loach 8cm
Botia birdi (Chaudhuri) 1909
Range: Punjab, North India

Golden Banded Loach 14cm
Botia dario (Hamilton-Buchanan) 1822
Range: Assam, Bengal and Bihar

Twin Banded Loach 4cm
Botia rostrata (Gunther) 1868
Range: Assam

Striped Loach 6cm
Botia striata (Rao) 1920
Range: Tunga River system and Kolhapur, Satara Dist, Maharashtra

Shovelmouth Catfish 200cm
Aorichthys aor (Hamilton-Buchanan) 1822
Range: throughout India

Shovelnose Catfish 180cm
Aorichthys seenghala (Sykes) 1841
Range: throughout India

Translucent Catfish 10cm
Batasio batasio (Hamilton-Buchanan) 1822
Range: West Bengal and Assam

Assamese Mottled Catfish 9cm
Batasio tengana (Hamilton-Buchanan) 1822
Range: Upper Assam

White Collared Imperial Catfish 35cm
Horabagrus nigri collaris (Pethyagoda and
Kotellat) 1991
Range: Kerala

Bleeker's Catfish 13.5cm
Mystus bleekeri (Day) 1846
Range: Northern India

Long Whiskered Catfish 40cm
Mystus gulio (Hamilton-Buchanan) 1822
Range: coastal areas of India

Grey Catfish 12.5cm
Mystus keletius (Valenciennes) 1839
Range: Karnataka

Menoda Catfish 40cm
Mystus menoda (Hamilton-Buchanan) 1822
Range: Orissa

Guinea Catfish 8cm
Mystus tengara (Hamilton-Buchanan) 1822
Range: Eastern India

Pyjama Striped Catfish 16cm
Mystus vittatus (Bloch) 1797
Range: throughout India

Headstander Catfish 15cm
Chandramara chandramara (Hamilton-Buchanan) 1822
Range: North Bengal, Assam

Velvet Catfish 36cm
Rita pavimentatus (Valenciennes) 1832
Range: Andhra Pradesh

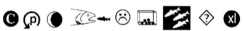

Butter Catfish 45cm
Ompok bimaculatus (Bloch) 1797
Range: throughout India

Gulper Catfish 17cm
Ompok pabda (Hamilton-Buchanan) 1822
Range: North-east India

Killer Catfish 250cm
Wallago attu (Schneider) 1801
Range: throughout India

Striped Glass Catfish 8cm
Pseudeutropius atherinoides (Bloch) 1794
Range: throughout India

Indian Tiger Shark 150cm
Pangasius pangasius (Hamilton-Buchanan) 1822
Range: large rivers and estuaries of India

Giant River Catfish 250cm
Bagarius yarelli (Sykes) 1841
Range: throughout India

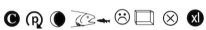

Thread Tail Catfish 7.8cm
Conta conta (Hamilton-Buchanan) 1822
Range Upper Assam

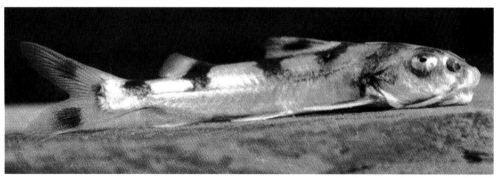

Clown Catfish 10cm
Gagata cenia (Hamilton-Buchanan) 1822
Range: North and North East India

Black Line Catfish 18cm
Glyptothorax anamaliensis (Silas) 1951
Range: Base of Anamalai Hills, Kerala

Banded Torrent Catfish 8cm
Glyptothorax cavia (Hamilton-Buchanan) 1822
Range: Eastern India

Bronze Catfish 10cm
Glyptothorax brevipinnis (Hora) 1923
Range: Upper Assam

Belly Sucker Catfish 8cm
Glyptothorax coheni (Ganguly Datta and Sen) 1972
Range: Subarnarekha River, Bihar

Copper Catfish 8cm
Glyptothorax telchitta (Hamilton-Buchanan) 1822
Range: Northern India

Butterfly Catfish 5cm
Hara hara (Hamilton-Buchanan) 1822
Range: North and North-east India

Elongated Moth Catfish 2cm
Hara horai (Misra) 1950
Range: North Bengal (Terai and Duars)

Dwarf Anchor Catfish 2cm
Hara jerdoni (Day) 1870
Range: North-east India

Giant Moth Catfish 10cm
Hara filamentosa (Blyth) 1861
Range: Dibru River, Assam

Bee Catfish 4cm
Laguvia kapuri (Tilak and Hussain) 1974
Range: Padhoi River at Saharanpur, Uttar Pradesh

Ribero's Catfish 6cm
Laguvia riberoi (Hora) 1921
Range: Teesta River system, North Bengal

Cheetah Catfish 3cm
Laguvia shawi (Hora) 1921
Range: Teesta Drainage, Darjeeling Himalayas, North Bengal

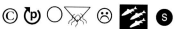

Broad Headed Catfish 8.5cm
Nangra viridescens (Hamilton-Buchanan) 1822
Range: Assam

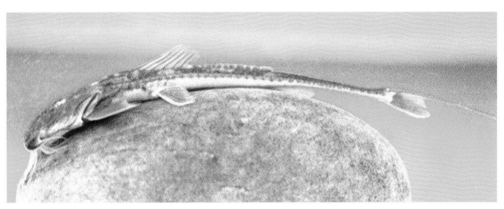

Whiptail Catfish 18cm
Sisor rhabdophorus (Hamilton-Buchanan) 1822
Range: Assam and Bihar

Asian Stinging Catfish 30cm
Heteropneustes fossilis (Bloch) 1794
Range: throughout India

Devil Catfish 20cm
Chaca chaca (Hamilton-Buchanan) 1822
Range: West Bengal, Bihar and Assam

Long Fighting Catfish 11cm
Olyra longicaudata (McClelland) 1842
Range: Upper Assam

Fighting Catfish 7cm
Olyra horai (Prashad and Mukerji) 1929
Range: Meghalaya

Dusky Shark Catfish 60cm
Arius sona (Hamilton-Buchanan) 1822
Range: Gangetic Delta, Sunderbans, West Bengal

Spotted Shark Catfish 20cm
Arius maculatus
Range: Hoogly Estuary

Eel Catfish 150cm
Plotosus canius (Hamilton-Buchanan) 1822
Range: Matla River, Sunderbans

Toad Fish 30cm
Batrichthys grunniens (Linnaeus) 1758
Range: coastal areas of Eastern India

Red Half Beak 7.5cm
Dermogenys pusillus (Van Hasselt) 1823
Range: Hoogly Estuary, West Bengal

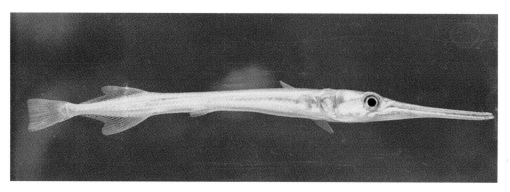

Long Nosed Needle Fish 30cm
Xenentodon cancila (Hamilton-Buchanan) 1822
Range: most of India

Blue Eyes 2.5cm
Oryzias melastima (McClelland) 1839
Range: throughout India

Striped Panchax 6cm
Aplocheilus lineatus (Valenciennes) 1846
Range: Western and Southern regions of India

Red Panchax 4cm
Aplocheilus panchax (Hamilton-Buchanan) 1822
Range: North and Eastern India

Day's Panchax 4cm
Aplocheilus dayi (Steindachner) 1892
Range: Kerala

Jewel Panchax 2cm
Aplocheilus parvus (Sundara Raj) 1916
Range: Karnataka

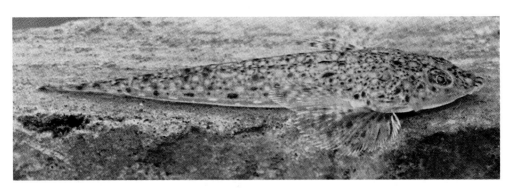

Jewelled Alligator Fish 8cm
Platycephalus bengalensis (? name, date)
Range: Matla River, West Bengal

Giant Sea Perch 60cm
Lates calcarifer (Bloch) 1790
Range: Indo-West Pacific

Bald Glassy Perchlet 10cm
Ambassis gymnocephalus (Lacepede) 1802
Range: Vembanad and Pulicat Lakes of Kerala

Himalayan Glass Perchlet 5cm
Pseudambassis baculis (Hamilton-Buchanan) 1822
Range: Himalayan and Indo-Gangetic Plains

High Fin Glassfish 3cm
Pseudambassis ranga (Hamilton-Buchanan) 1822
Range: throughout India

Giant Glassfish 12cm
Parambassis thomassi (Day) 1870
Range: Western Ghats of Kerala and Karnatka

Aerial Fish 36cm
Sillaginopsis panijus (Hamilton-Buchanan) 1822
Range: southwest coast, east coast, Gangetic Delta

Mangrove Red Snapper 12cm
Lutjanus argentimaculatus (Forsskal) 1775
Range: Indo-West Pacific

Round Perch 15cm
Lutjanus kishorii (Rao) 1997
Range: Hooghli-Matla Estuary, West Bengal

Six Banded Tiger 16cm
Datnioides quadrifasciatus (Sevastianov) 1809
Range: Sunderbans, West Bengal

Finger Fish 6cm
Monodactylus argenteus (Linnaeus) 1758
Range: Indo West Pacific

Spotted Scat 30cm
Scatophagus argus argus (Linnaeus) 1766
Range: coastal estuaries of India

Red Scat 20cm
Scatophagus argus rubrifrons (Sterba) 1963
Range: Hooghly Estuary, West Bengal

Leaffish 16cm
Nandus nandus (Hamilton-Buchanan) 1822
Range: throughout India

Yellow Sunfish 15cm
Pristolepis marginata (Jerdon) 1848
Range: Kerala

Orange Chromide 5cm
Etroplus maculatus (Bloch) 1785
Range: Southern India

Malabar Sunfish 8cm
Pristolepis malabarica (Gunther)
Range: Western Ghats

Dwarf Chameleon 4cm
Badis badis badis (Hamilton-Buchanan) 1822
Range: north and eastern parts of India

Red Chameleon Fish 8cm
Badis badis burmanicus (Ahl) 1936
Range: Upper Assam

Pearl Spot cm 8cm
Etroplus suratensis (Bloch) 1785
Range: Southern India

Banded Chromide 8cm
Etroplus canarensis (Day) 1877
Range: Western Karnataka

Mozambique Mouthbreeder 18cm
Oreochromis mossambica (Peters) 1852
Range: introduced

Silver Mullet 25cm
Liza parsia (Hamilton-Buchanan) 1822
Range: coastal waters of India

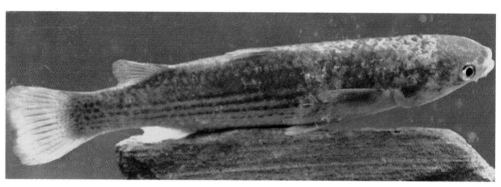

Grey Mullet 36cm
Liza tade (Forsskal) 1775
Range: coastal waters of India

Indian Anableps 25cm
Rinomugil corsula (Hamilton-Buchanan) 1822
Range: Hooghly-Matla and Mahanadi Estuary

Sleeper Goby 30cm
Glossogobius giuris (Hamilton-Buchanan) 1822
Range: freshwaters of Eastern India

Black Faced Neon Goby 5cm
In press (Rao) 1997
Range: Sunderbans, West Bengal

Moustached Sailfin Goby 9cm
Oligolepis acutipennis (Valenciennes) 1837
Range: Sunderbans, West Bengal

Knight Goby 6cm
Stigmatogobius sadanundio (Hamilton-Buchanan) 1822
Range: Hooghly Estuary, Eastern India

Scary Dragon 15cm
Apocryptes bato (Hamilton-Buchanan) 1822
Range: estuaries of Eastern India

Blue Spot Dragon 12cm
Boleophthalmus boddarti (Pallas) 1770
Range: Coastal mudflats of India

Banded Goby 18cm
Pseudapocryptes lanceolatus (Block and Schneider) 1801
Range: Hooghly Estuary, West Bengal

Multispotted Neon Goby 8cm
Gobiopterus chuno (Hamilton-Buchanan) 1822
Range: Hooghly-Matla Estuary, West Bengal

Clown Goby 8cm
Sicyopterus griseus (Day) 1876
Range: South Karnataka

Duckbill Goby 8cm
Butis butis (Hamilton-Buchanan) 1822
Range: Indo-West Pacific

Dusky Goby 17cm
Eleotris fusca (Schneider) 1801
Range: Indo-West Pacific

Bicolor Goby 7cm
Eleotris melanosoma (Bleeker) 1852
Range: tropical Indo-West Pacific

Armadillo Goby 6cm
Odonteleotris macrodon (Bleeker) 1853
Range: West Bengal

Climbing Perch 10cm
Anabas testudineus (Bloch) 1795
Range: almost throughout India

Noble Gourami 10cm
Ctenops nobilis (McClelland) 1845
Range: Eastern India

127

Spike Tailed Paradise Fish 4cm
Pseudosphromenus cupanus dayi (Kohler) 1909
Range: Kerala

Striped Gourami 12cm
Colisa fasciata (Schneider) 1801
Range: Eastern India

Dwarf Gourami 3cm
Colisa lalia (Hamilton-Buchanan) 1822
Range: throughout India

Honey Gourami 4cm
Colisa sota (Hamilton-Buchanan) 1822
Range: North-east India

Bhutan Snakehead 20cm
Channa amphibius (McClelland) 1845
Range: North Bengal, foothills of the Bhutan Hills

Spotted Snakehead 30cm
Channa barca (Hamilton-Buchanan) 1822
Range: Assam

129

Peacock Snakehead 122cm
Channa marulius marulius
(Hamilton-Buchanan) 1822
Range: throughout India

Issabella Snakehead 46cm
Channa marulius issabella (Rao) 1997
Range: throughout India

Bengal Snakehead 15cm
Channa orientalis (Hamilton-Buchanan) 1822
Range: Eastern India

Broad Banded Snakehead 20cm
Channa umangii (Rao) 1997
Rane: Eastern Ghats, Orissa

Indian Snakehead 30cm
Channa punctata (Bloch) 1793
Range: throughout India

Georgette Snakehead 16cm
Channa stewarti (Playfair) 1867
Range: Upper Assam

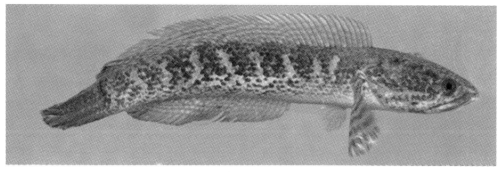

Cobra Snakehead 30cm
Channa harcourt-butleri (Annandale) 1918
Range: North Lakhimpur, Assam

Striped Snakehead 60cm
Channa striatus (Bloch) 1793
Range: throughout India

Rainbow Snakehead 20cm
Channa bleheri (Vierke) 1991
Range: Upper Assam

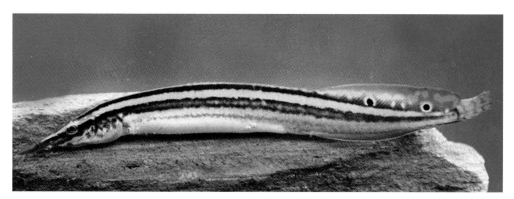

Peacock Eel 30cm
Macrognathus aral (Bloch and Schneider) 1801
Range: Eastern India

Red Tailed Eel 30cm
Macrognathus jacobbi (Rao) 1997
Range: North Bengal

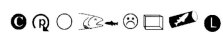

Spiny Green Eel 15cm
Mastacembelus pancalus (Hamilton-Buchanan) 1822
Range: throughout India

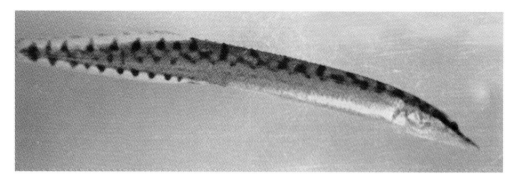

Tyre Track Eel 60cm
Mastacembelus armatus (Lacepede) 1800
Range: India

Topaz Puffer 17cm
Chelonodon steindachneri (? name, date)
Range: Hooghly Estuary

Burmese Puffer 15cm
Chelonodon nigroviridis (Proce) 1822
Range: Gangetic Delta and eastwards

White Spotted Puffer 20cm
Chelonodon patoca (Hamilton-Buchanan) 1822
Range: tropical Indo-West Pacific

Emerald Puffer 6cm
Tetraodon cutcutia (Hamilton-Buchanan) 1822
Range: north and eastern India

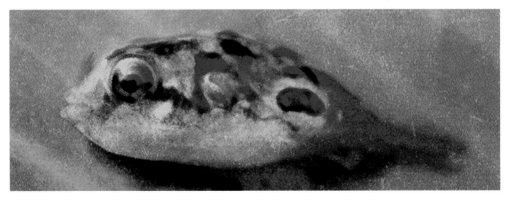

Red Greed Dwarf Puffer 2cm
Monotretus travancoricus (Hora and Nair) 1941
Range: Kerala and Karnataka

Glossary

Abdomen:	belly.
Adipose:	a small and fleshy fin, without rays, placed behind the dorsal fin on the back of some fishes.
Aerial:	belonging to the air or atmosphere.
Airbladder (gas bladder):	a gas-filled sac located in the body cavity below the vertebrae.
Algae:	a huge group of Thallophytes, the seaweeds and allied forms.
Amphibious:	living or adapted to life or use, on land and in or on water.
Anal Fin:	the impaired fin on the midline of the underside of the body, just behind the vent.
Anatomy:	the science of the structure of the animal body.
Anoxic:	deficient supply of oxygen to the tissues.
Aphrodisiacs:	that which encourages sexual excitement or performance.
Arborescent:	growing, formed, branched like a tree.
Archipelago:	a sea abounding in islands or a group of islands.
Barbels:	a slender, tactile, whisker-like projection extending from the head of some fishes; they function primarily as a sensory organ for locating food.
Base:	the part where a fin joins body, as in length of dorsal/anal fin base.
Bay:	an inlet of the sea with a wider opening than a gulf, an inward bend.
Benthic:	sea-bottom dwellers.
Bifid:	cleft in two.
Brackish:	a mix of salt and fresh water.
Branchial:	pertaining to gills.
Capillaries:	a minute vessel such as those that connect arteries with veins.
Cartilaginous:	firm, elastic tissue, softer than bone, which forms the skeletal structure of sharks and rays.
Catadromous:	descending periodically for spawning to the lower parts of a river or to the sea.
Caudal fin:	the tail fin.
Cavernicolous:	prefers to stay in caverns or cavities.
Circumglobal:	around the world.
Column:	a long round body.
Crenulated:	finely notched.
Cycloid scale:	a smooth-edged, more or less circular scale with concentric striations.
Cyclopsidal:	fish which which have an eye in front and eat minute freshwater copepods.
Deltaic:	belonging to a delta.
Detritus:	an aggregate of loosened fragments.
Dimorphic:	occurrence of two forms in the same species.
Disc:	the flat, more or less rounded part of rays which consists of the body and pectoral fins.
Dorsal fin:	the back or upper part of the body: opposite to 'ventral'.
Ecology:	the study of plants and animals.
Endemic:	confined to the particular area.
Estuarine:	the inhabitants of a wide lower tidal part of a river.
Fissures:	a narrow opening or chasm.
Icththyologists:	specialists in the branch of natural history that is the study of fishes.
Isinglass:	a material, mainly gelatine, obtained from the air-bladder of certain fishes.
Isthmus:	anterior portion of breast of fishes, generally pointed forward dividing the two gill openings below and serving in part, to attach the mandible to body.
Labial:	formed by the lips.
Lacustrine:	pertaining to lakes, dwelling in lakes.
Larvae:	young of insects in the first stage of development.
Larvivorous:	fish that eat the young (larvae) of insects.
Lateral:	belonging to the side.
Mandibular:	pertaining to the lower jaw bones.
Maxillary:	in fishes, a bone included in the upper jaw.
Meristic:	repetition of parts.
Migration:	to change habitat periodically.
Monoganous:	sticking to one mate for life.
Monotypic:	a species forming a genus by itself.

Montane:	mountain dwelling.
Morphology:	the science of form, especially that of the outer form, inner structure, and development of living organisms and their parts.
Mucous:	the slimy fluid secreted by the mucous membrane.
Nape:	the upper neck region.
Niche:	a suitable or actual place or the system of nature.
Nomenclature:	a system of names.
Oceanic:	pertaining to the ocean; found or formed in the oceans or high seas.
Organ:	a part of a body capable of carrying on a natural or vital operation.
Oriental:	pertaining to, or from the East: an Asiatic.
Osseus:	bony.
Osteological:	pertaining to the study of bones, part of anatomy.
Papillated:	pertaining to small nipple like protuberances, minute elevations of the skin.
Pectoral:	pertaining to the breast or shoulder.
Pelagic:	living in open water in contrast to the bottom or inshore.
Pelvic:	pertaining to the pelvis or pelvic girdle.
Pendulous:	hanging loosely, swinging freely.
Peninsula:	a piece of land that is almost an island.
Percoid:	affinity with the perch family.
Pigmentation:	colouration or discolouration by pigments in the tissue.
Pituitary gland:	a ductless gland at the base of the brain that affects growth.
Polar:	pertaining to the North and South Poles areas.
Polyphyletic:	multiple origin.
Pores:	very small openings or holes pierced into the skin.
Pouch:	any pocket-like structure.
Predator:	something that lives on other forms of life.
Preopercle:	bones of side surface of head, situated before the gill cover or opercle.
Proboscis:	a trunk or long snout; a trunk-like process, as the suctorial mouth parts of some insects.
Progeny:	offspring.
Protractile:	capable of being thrust forward.
Pugnacious:	given to fighting.
Regression:	backward movement or extension.
Riverine:	only inhabiting rivers.
Rivulets:	a small river or stream.
Rostral:	of or like a rostrum.
Rostrum:	a beak.
Saline:	salty.
Scute:	an external horny or bony plate or scale.
Sensory:	of sensation.
Serrated:	with sharp, forward-pointing teeth.
Snout:	the part of the head in front of the eyes.
Spawn:	mass of eggs laid in water.
Spinous:	spiny.
Sporadic:	occurring occasionally.
Swimbladder:	a fish's airbladder.
Systematics:	a set of things considered as a connected whole.
Taxonomy:	the science of classification at all levels starting with the individual and arranging or grouping according to relationships.
Temperate:	moderate in temperature.
Thoracic:	pertaining to the thorax or chest.
Translucent:	imperfectly transparent.
Trunk:	the body of an animal apart from head and limbs.
Tubercles:	protuberance or swelling.
Velocity:	rate of change of position.
Ventral:	situated on the abdomen of animals; the opposite of dorsal.
Viviparous:	producing live young instead of eggs.
Vomerine:	bone in mid-palate, often bearing teeth.
Voracious:	eating greedily or in large quantities.

Bibliography

Axelrod, H.R., Emmens, C.W., Scuthorpe, D., Vorderwinkler, W. and Pronek, N. (1967) *Exotic Tropical Fishes*. TFH Publications, Jersey City, USA. 608 pp.

Banarescu, P. (1968) Revision of the Indo-Burmese genus Salmostoma Swainson (Pisces, Cyprinidae) with description of a new subspecies. *Revue roum. Biol. (Zool.)*, **13(1)** 3–14.

Banarescu, P. (1972) The zoogeographical position of the East Asian freshwater fish fauna. *Revue roum. Biol. (Zool.)*, **17(5)** 315–23.

Banarescu, P. (1986) A review of the species of Crossocheilus, Epalzeorhynchos and Paracrossochilus (Pisces, Cyprinidae). *Trav. Mus. Hist. Natn. Gr. Antipa*, **28** 141–61.

Barlow, G.W., Liem, K.F. and Wickler, W. (1968) Badidae, a new fish family – behavorial, osteological and developmental evidence. *J. Zool.* London, **156** 415–47.

Barman, R.P. (1984) Biosystematic studies of the cyprinid fishes of the genus *Danio* Hamilton from the Indian region with a discussion of the Subfamily Rasborinae.Ph.D. Thesis. University of Calcutta.

Castle, P.H.J. (1968) A contribution to the revision of the Moringuid eels. *Spec. Publ. Dept. Ichthyol.* Rhodes University, **(13)** 1–29.

Dadyburjor, S.J. (1955) Breeding habits of a new fish Laubuca dadyburjori from Cochin. *Bull. Bombay Aquar. Soc.*, **3(1/2)** 12–13.

David, A. (1952) New records of Himalayan fishes in the Damodar and Mahanadi river systems. *Sci. & Cult.*, **17(2)** 528.

Day, F. (1875–78) The Fishes of India: being a natural history of the fishes known to inhabit the seas and fresh waters of India, Burma and Ceylon. Text and Atlas in 4 parts. London, xx + 778 pp., 195 pls. (Issued in 4 parts; for dating see Whitehead and Talwar, 1976.)

Day, F. (1888) *Fishes of India*. Supplement, October, 1888. William Dawson, London, 779–816.

Day, F. (1889) *The Fauna of British India, including Ceylon and Burma. Fishes*, 1,548 pp; 2509 pp. London: Taylor and Francis.

Dekkers, W.J. (1975) Review of the Asiatic freshwater puffers of the genus Tetraodon Linnaeus, 1758 (Pisces, Tetraodontiformes, Tetraodontidae). *Bijdr. Dierk.*, **45(1)** 87–142.

Frank, S. and Franke, H. (1963) A new Brachydanio. *Tropical Fish Hobbyist* (June 1963) 61–62.

Haig, J. (1951) Studies on the classification of the catfishes of the Oriental and Palaearctic family *Siluridae*. *Rec. Indian Mus.*, **48(3/4)** 59–116.

Hamilton-Buchanan, F. (1822) *An account of the fishes found in the river Ganges and its branches*. Edinburgh and London. vii + 405 pp + 39 pls.

Hora, S.L. (1921) Indian cyprinoid fishes belonging to the genus Garra with notes on related species from other countries. *Rec. Indian Mus.*, **22(5)** 633–87.

Hora, S.L. (1937) The game fishes of India. I. The Indian trout, *Barilius (Opsarius) bola* (Hamilton). *J. Bombay Nat. Hist. Soc.*, **39(2)** 199–210.

Hora, S.L. (1939a) The game fishes of India. VI. The goonch, *Bagarius bagarius* (Hamilton). *J. Bombay Nat. Hist. Soc.*, **40(4)** 583–93.

Hora, S.L. (1939b) The game fishes of India. VII. The Mahseers or the largescaled Barbels of India. 1. The Putitor mahseer, *Barbus (Tor) putitora* (Hamilton). *J. Bombay Nat. Hist. Soc.*, **41(2)** 272–85.

Hora, S.L. (1940) On a collection of fish from the headwaters of the Mahanadi river, Raipur district, C.P.*Rec. Indian Mus.*, **42(2)** 365–74.

Hora, S.L. (1950) Siluroid fishes of India, Burma and Ceylon. XIII. Fishes of the genera Erethistes Muller and Troschel, Hara Blyth and two allied genera. *Rec. Indian Mus.*, **47(2)** 183–201.

Howes, G.J. (1980a) The anatomy, phylogeny and classification of the bariliine cyprinid fishes. *Bull. Br. Mus. Nat. Hist. (Zool.)*, **37(3)** 129–98.

Howes, G.J. (1980b) A new genus of cheline cyprinid fishes. *Bull. Br. Mus. Nat. Hist. (Zool.)*, **38(3)** 171–73.

Howes, G.J. (1983) Additional notes on bariliine cyprinid fishes. *Bull. Br. Mus. Nat. Hist. (Zool.)*, **45(2)** 95–101.

Innes, W.T. (1935) *Exotic Aquarium Fishes*. Innes Publications, Philadelphia, USA. 400 pp.

Jayaram, K.C. (1977) Aid to identification of siluroid fishes of India, Burma, Sri Lanka, Pakistan and Bangladesh. I. Bagridae. *Rec. Zool. Surv. India* Occ. Paper, **(8)** 1–41.

Jayaram, K.C. (198) The Freshwater Fishes of India, Pakistan, Bangladesh, Burma and Sri Lanka. *Handbook Zoological Survey of India*, No. 2. xii + 475 pp.

Jayaram, K.C. (1982) Aid to the identification of the siluroid fishes of India, Burma, Sri Lanka, Pakistan and Bangladesh. 5. Ariidae and Plotosidae. *Rec. Zool. Surv. India* Occ. Paper, **(37)** 1–41.

Jhingran, V.G. (1982) *Fish and fisheries of India.* Hindustan Publishing Corporation, Delhi. 666pp.

Menon, A.G.K. (1963) Taxonomy of the Indian frog-fishes (Fam. *Batrachoididae*). *Labdev. Journ. Sci. & Tech.*, **1** 1–2.

Menon, A.G.K. (1966) Gambusia and mosquito control. *J.Bombay Nat Hist. Soc.*, **62(3)** 567–568.

Menon, A.G.K. (1977) Fish and malaria control. *Sci. & Cult.*, **43(3)** 110–14.

Menon, A.G.K. (1987) *Fauna of India and the adjacent countries.* Pisces, 4 (Part I). *Homalopteridae.* Calcutta. x + 259 pp.

Menon, A.G.K. and Jayaram, K.C. (1977) The freshwater grey mullet Rhinomugil corsula (Hamilton) as a fishery resource in the Cauvery river system, *S.India. Sci. & Cult.*, **43(7)** 302–304.

Mukerji, D.D. (1931) On a small collection of fish from the Bhavani river (S.India). *J. Bombay Ñat. Hist. Soc.*, **35(1)** 162–71.

Myers, G.S. (1953) Classification of the *Danios. Aquar. J.*, **24(10)** 235–238.

Nelson, J.S. (1984) *Fishes of the World.* John Wiley and Sons, New York. 523 pp.

Rainboth, W.J. (1983) Psilorhynchus gracilis, a new cyprinoid fish from the Gangetic lowlands. *Proc. Calif. Acad. Sci.*, **43(6)** 67–76.

Rainboth, W.J. 1986. Fishes of the Asian cyprinid genus Chagunius. Occ. Paper Museum of Zoology, University of Michigan, **(712)** 1–17.

Rao, B.V.S. (1986) Systematic studies on *Anabas testudineus* (Bloch, 1792) and *A. oligolepis* Bleeker, 1855. *Proc. Indian Acad. Sci.*, **57(5)** 207–14.

Reddy, W.P.B. (1981) Studies on the taxonomy of Indian species of the family Channidae (Pisces: *Teleostei*) and some aspects of the biology of Channa punctata (Bloch, 1793) from Guntur, Andhra Pradesh, Ph.D. Thesis, Andhra University.

Roberts, T.R. (1983) Revision of the south and southeast sisorid catfish genus *Bagarius*, with description of a new species from the Mekong, *Copeia*, **(2)** 435–45.

Roberts, T.R. (1986) Systematic review of the *Mastacembelidae* or Spiny Eels of Burma and Thailand, with description of two new species of *Macrognathus. Jap. J.Ichthyol.*, **33(2)** 95–109.

Rosen, D.H. (1964) The relationships and taxonomic position of the Halfbeaks, Killifishes, Silversides and their relatives. *Bull. Am. Mus. Nat. Hist.*, **127(5)** 219–67.

Saigal, B.N. (1960) Studies on the fishery and biology of the commercial catfishes of the Ganga river system. II. Maturity, spawning and food of *Mystus* (Osteobagrus) *aor* (Ham.). *Indian J. Fish.*, **11(1)** 1–44.

Sane, S.R. and Chapgar, B.F. (1983) Extension of range of danio, Chela (Neochela) dadiburjori (Menon) (Pisces: Cyprinidae). *J.Bombay Nat. Hist. Soc.*, **80(1)** 232–34.

Sen, T.K. (1985) The fish fauna of Assam and the neighbouring north-eastern states of India. *Rec. Zool. Surv. India* Occ. Paper, **(64)** 1–216.

Shaw, C.E. and Shebbeare, E.O. (1937) The fishes of Northern Bengal. *J.Roy. Asiat. Soc. Beng.*, (Sci.), **3(1)** 1–137.

Silas, E.G. (1958) Studies on the cyprinid fishes of the Oriental genus Chela Hamilton. *J. Bombay Nat. Hist. Soc.*, **55(1)** 54–99.

Suter, M. (1941) Observations on the breeding colouration of Barbus (Puntius) kolus Sykes. *J. Bombay Nat. Hist. Soc.*, **43(3)** 407–408.

Talwar, P.K. (1984) in: Talwar, P.K. and Kacker, R.K. *Commercial Sea Fishes of India.* Handbook Zoological Survey of India No. 4. Lii + 997 pp.

Tilak, R. (1987) The Fauna of India and adjacent countries. Pisces (Teleostomi): Subfamily Schizothoracinae. Calcutta. x + 229 pp.

Travers, R.A. (1984a) A review of the Mastacembeloidei, a suborder of synbranchiform teleost fishes. Part I. *Bull. Br. Mus. Nat. Hist. (Zool.)*, **46(1)** 1–133.

Travers, R.A. (1984b) A review of the Mastacembeloidei, a suborder of synbranchiform teleost fishes. Part II. Phylogenetic analysis. *Bull. Br. Mus. Nat. Hist. (Zool.)*, **47(2)** 83–150.

Yazdani, G.M. (1977) On a new record of black ruby, Puntius nigrofasciatus (Gunther) from India (Cypriniformes: Cyprinidae). *Curr. Sci.*, **46(21)** 760.

Yazdani, G.M. (1978) Adaptive radiation in mastacemebeloid fishes. *Bull. Zool. Surv. India*, **1(3)** 279–90.

Index

The following index lists each fish that appears in Chapter 3,
together with the corresponding page number.

R

S